LOUISIANA
BUSINESS
CERTIFICATIONS
GUIDEBOOK

LOUISIANA BUSINESS CERTIFICATIONS GUIDEBOOK

Written by
Norman David Roussell, MBA

Published by

Start Smart, LLC, is the publisher of the website, www.CertAssist.net, and the *Louisiana Business Certifications Guidebook*. Information, contained on the website and in the guidebook, is from agency websites and other sources. All of the information was edited for this publication. This publication is designed to provide the reader with information and guidance about the subject matter covered. Neither the author nor the publisher is engaged in rendering legal, accounting or other professional services through this publication. The reader acknowledges that the information provided herein may change over time and, if additional research, legal or other expert advice is required, the reader should conduct additional research or retain the services of a competent expert. The author specifically disclaims responsibility for any liability, loss or risk incurred directly or indirectly from the contents of this guidebook. All trade names, trademarks or service marks that appear in this book are trade names, trademarks or service marks of their respective holders.

TABLE OF CONTENTS

TABLE OF CONTENTS (CONT'D)

Dear Reader,

I am excited to introduce the latest edition of the *Louisiana Business Certifications Guidebook*. As the owner of a certified DBE/MBE/SBE firm, I understand that certification applications can be tricky and certification programs can be difficult to understand. That is why I have applied my years of certification consulting and training expertise to writing this comprehensive, yet easy-to-understand, introduction to business certification programs available to Louisiana businesses.

Business certification programs exist to level the playing field and give all businesses, including small, disadvantaged, minority, women-owned and veteran-owned businesses, an equal opportunity to bid, win and perform on government and private sector contracts.

In conjunction with our www.CertAssist.net website, the *Louisiana Business Certifications Guidebook* is a valuable tool to help Louisiana businesses succeed.

Good luck!

Sincerely,

Norman David Roussell, MBA
Author & CEO of Start Smart, LLC

WWW.CERTASSIST.NET

2006 2016

~

When you awake in the morning, ask yourself:
What can I do today towards achieving my goals?

At noon, ask yourself:
Am I doing what I need to do today towards achieving my goals?

Before you go to sleep at night, ask yourself:
Did I do everything possible today towards achieving my goals?

~

FAITH. PERSEVERANCE. FORTITUDE.
I am an entrepreneur!

CERTIFICATION FAQs

Q: What does the term 'DBE' mean?
A: The term 'DBE' is the acronym for *Disadvantaged Business Enterprise*. A DBE is a business that is owned, managed and controlled by a socially and economically disadvantaged individual. (See page 5 for the definitions of socially disadvantaged and economically disadvantaged).

Q: Why were DBE programs created?
A: DBE programs were created to ensure non-discrimination in the award and administration of government-funded and private sector contracts and to create a level playing field on which all businesses can compete for contracting opportunities.

Q: Does every state have a DBE certification program?
A: All Federal Highway Administration and U.S. Department of Transportation (DOT) recipients of funding that award contracts totaling over $250,000 per year are required to participate in the DOT's Unified Certification Program.

Q: Is my business automatically a DBE since I am a woman and a minority?
A: Being a member of a specific group may qualify your firm to be a DBE, but it does not automatically mean your business is a DBE. Use of the term DBE typically involves a certification process and recognition by a certifying agency that your firm has met the requirements for certification as a DBE.

Q: What does it mean to perform a "commercially useful function"?
A: A business performs a commercially useful function if it:

- Is responsible for the execution of a distinct element of the work on a contract;
- Carries out its obligation by actually performing managing or supervising the work involved;
- Performs work that is normal for its business, services and function; and
- Is not further subcontracting a portion of the work that is greater than that expected to be subcontracted by normal industry practices.

Q: What is the purpose of the commercially useful function requirement?
A: The purpose of the commercially useful function requirement is to prevent certified DBE businesses from acting as a "pass through" or "front company" when identified as the prime bidder or subcontractor. The commercially useful function requirement is in place to prevent artificial, incidental or even non-existent participation by a DBE firm to meet the DBE goal of a contract. Only businesses that perform a commercially useful function can qualify for DBE certification.

Q: Can a non-profit become a certified DBE?
A: Non-profit organizations are controlled by a Board of Directors and cannot be certified as a DBE, MBE or SBE.

Q: Can I apply for certification as a woman-owned business if I am married?
A: Louisiana is a community property state. As a result, you and your husband would need a legally binding separate property agreement and the company's articles, bylaws or operating agreement would have to show that you own at least 51% of the business. Additionally, you will have to prove, through the application, supporting documents and on-site visit, that you manage and control the business in order for the business to be certified as a woman-owned business.

Q: What are the requirements for DBE certification?
A: Requirements vary depending on the certification program and certifying agency. Requirements for certification are included with the information on each program included in this guidebook.

Q: Why do I need to register with Dun & Bradstreet?
A: Any business that wants to do business with the U.S. government is required to register with Dun & Bradstreet (DNB) and obtain a DNB D-U-N-S Number. A D-U-N-S Number is a unique nine-digit number assigned to a business. The U.S. government uses the D-U-N-S Number as part of its business verification process when a business registers as a vendor in the System for Award Management.

Q: What is the System for Award Management?
A: Any business that wants to do business with the U.S. government must register with the System for Award Management (SAM). SAM is a Federal government owned and operated website that consolidates the information contained in CCR/FedReg, ORCA, and EPLS. SAM is now the primary database of vendors that provide goods and services to the U.S. government.

Q: What documents do I need to apply for certification?
A: The supporting documents you need to include with your certification application vary depending on the certification program and certifying agency. There is a *Sample Checklist of Supporting Documents* on page 68 with a list of the most commonly requested supporting documents for certification programs.

Q: What is Title VI of the Civil Rights Act?
A: Title VI, 42 U.S.C. § 2000d et seq., was enacted as part of the Civil Rights Act of 1964. It prohibits discrimination on the basis of race, color, and national origin in programs and activities receiving Federal financial assistance. If a business owner believes he/she has been denied a contracting opportunity on the basis of race, color or national origin, the owner can file a discrimination complaint against the agency that denied the opportunity.

Q: What is a "First Tier or Second Tier" subcontractor?
A: A first-tier subcontractor holds a subcontract with a prime contractor. A second-tier contractor subcontracts with a first-tier subcontractor and so forth.

Q: Can a franchise become a certified DBE?
A: Only an independent business may be certified as a DBE. In determining whether a franchise is an independent business, the certifying agency will review the applicant firm's relationship with the franchisor, in such areas as personnel, facilities, equipment, financial and other resources. If it is determined that the franchise does not depend too heavily on its relationship with the franchisor for its viability, the franchise may be considered for certification as a DBE. Keep in mind that some certification programs will not allow a franchise to become a certified DBE under any circumstances. Contact the certifying agency for clarification on this topic prior to submitting an application for certification.

Q: What are the Federal government's goals for contracting with small businesses?
A: Formal goals are in place to ensure that small businesses get their fair share of work with the Federal government. In fact, each Federal agency must set an annual goal for participation in its contracts by various groups. Below is a sampling of the statutory goals[*] established by Federal executive agencies:

- 23% of prime contracts for small businesses;
- 5% of prime and subcontracts for women-owned small businesses;
- 5% of prime contracts and subcontracts for Small Disadvantaged Businesses;
- 3% of prime contracts and subcontracts for HUBZone small businesses; and
- 3% of prime and subcontracts for service-disabled veteran-owned small businesses.

[*]SOURCE: http://www.sba.gov/content/small-business-goaling

Only apply for certification with programs that align with your overall business goals. For example, if your company's goal is to operate in a local market, applying to become a Government Services Administration (GSA) Schedule Contractor may not be the best fit.

KEY DEFINITIONS

Socially Disadvantaged
Socially disadvantaged individuals are those who have been subjected to racial or ethnic prejudice or cultural bias because of their identity as a member of a group without regard to their individual qualities.

Economically Disadvantaged
Economically disadvantaged individuals are those socially disadvantaged individuals whose ability to compete in the free enterprise system has been impaired due to diminished capital and credit opportunities as compared to others in the same business area that are not socially disadvantaged. In determining the degree of diminished credit and capital opportunities the certifying agencies typically consider, but not be limited to, the assets and net worth of such socially disadvantaged individuals.

Race-Conscious
Participation as a certified business is based on being a member of a specific ethnic group.

Race-Neutral
Participation as a certified business is not based on membership in an ethnic group, but typically is based on evidence of social and/or economic disadvantage of the owner(s).

Disadvantaged Business Enterprise
A disadvantaged business enterprise (DBE) is a business that is owned, managed and controlled by a socially and economically disadvantaged individual. The term DBE is a race-neutral term.

Small Business Enterprise
A small business enterprise (SBE) is a business that is classified as a small business based on U.S. SBA Size Standards.

Minority Business Enterprise
A Minority Business Enterprise (MBE) is a business that is at least 51% owned, managed and controlled by an ethnic minority.

Woman-Owned Business Enterprise
A Woman-Owned Business Enterprise (WBE) is a business that is at least 51% owned, managed and controlled by a woman.

Veteran-Owned Business
A Veteran-Owned Business (VOSB) is a business that is owned, managed and controlled by an individual who served and who was honorably discharged from the U.S. armed forces. A business owned by a disabled veteran is designated as a Service-Disabled Veteran-Owned Small Business (SDVOSB).

SBA Size Standards

SBA size standards represent the largest size that a business (including its subsidiaries and affiliates) may be to remain classified as a small business concern. In determining what constitutes a small business, the definition will vary to reflect industry differences. These size standards are used to determine eligibility for Federal government procurement programs designed to help small businesses and for designation as a certified SBE.

You can visit www.sba.gov/size to see if your business is considered a small business.

NAICS Code

The North American Industry Classification System (NAICS) was introduced in 1997 as a replacement for Standard Industrial Classification Codes (SIC). NAICS now serves as the standard for the three NAFTA countries of Mexico, Canada and the U.S. and is now the standard for use by Federal statistical agencies in classifying business establishments for the collection, analysis, and publication of statistical data related to the business economy of the U.S. The U.S. Census Bureau assigns and maintains only one NAICS code for each establishment based on its primary activity, though a business can have multiple NAICS codes.

Visit **www.Census.gov** to find your NAICS codes.

SIC Code

The Standard Industrial Classification (SIC) is a system for classifying industries by a four-digit code. Established in the United States in 1937, it is used by government agencies to classify industry areas.

NIGP Code

The NIGP Commodity/Services Code is an acronym for the National Institute of Governmental Purchasing (NIGP) Commodity Services Code. The NIGP Code is a coding system used primarily to classify products and services procured by state and local governments in the United States.

CSI Codes

Construction Specifications Institute (CSI) codes are the construction industry standard codes for specifications, estimates and product data.

GOVERNMENT PROCUREMENT ACRONYMS[1]

ACRONYM	DEFINITION
BOD	Bid Opening Date
CAGE	Commercial and Government Entity
CCR	Central Contractor Registration
CFR	Code of Federal Regulations
DBE	Disadvantaged Business Enterprise
DSMB	Dynamic Small Business Module
EDWOSB	Economically-Disadvantaged Woman-Owned Small Business
EIN	Employer Identification Number
DUNS	Data Universal Numbering System
FAC	Federal Acquisition Circular
EFT	Electronic Funds Transfer
FAR	Federal Acquisition Regulation
FSC	Federal Supply Classification
IDIQ	Indefinite Date, Indefinite Quantity
IFB	Invitation for Bid
HUBZONE	Historically Underutilized Business Zone
MBE	Minority Business Enterprise
MPIN	Marketing Partner Identification Number
NSN	National Stock Number
NAICS	North American Industry Classification System
ORCA	Online Representations and Certifications Application
NOFA	Notice of Funding Availability
PCR	Procurement Center Representative
PO	Purchase Order
PSC	Product Service Classification
PTAC	Procurement Technical Assistance Center
RFP	Request for Proposal
RFQ	Request for Qualifications
SADBU	Small and Disadvantaged Business Utilization
SAM	System for Award Management
SAT	Simplified Acquisition Threshold
[SBA] 8(a)	8(a) Business Development Program
SBE	Small Business Enterprise
SBIR	Small Business Innovation Research
SDB	Small Disadvantaged Business
SDVOSB	Service-Disabled Veteran-Owned Small Business
SF	Standard Form
SIC	Standard Industrial Classification
SOL	Solicitation
TPIN	Trading Partner Identification Number
VOSB	Veteran-Owned Small Business
WBE	Woman-Owned Business Enterprise
WOSB	Woman-Owned Small Business

[1]Sources: LA-PTAC.ORG, FBO.GOV and GSA.GOV.
The list above contains commonly used terms, but is not all-inclusive.

Review the *Checklist of Supporting Documents* for each program to ensure you have all of the documents required for certification such as résumés, tax returns and financial statements. See the *Sample Checklist of Supporting Documents* on page 66 for a list of supporting documents typically required for certification.

LOUISIANA UNIFIED CERTIFICATION PROGRAM
DISADVANTAGED BUSINESS ENTERPRISE

SUMMARY

CERTIFYING AGENCIES	**REGION 1:** LOUISIANA DEPARTMENT OF TRANSPORTATION **REGION 2:** LOUIS ARMSTRONG INTERNATIONAL AIRPORT NEW ORLEANS REGIONAL TRANSIT AUTHORITY ORLEANS LEVEE BOARD
DESIGNATION	DBE
RACE CONSCIOUS	NO
GENDER CONSCIOUS	NO
RECERTIFICATION	ANNUAL
GRADUATION	NONE
FEE/COST	NONE
CERTIFICATION TIMEFRAME	30-60 DAYS

OVERVIEW

The U.S. Department of Transportation's Disadvantaged Business Enterprise (DBE) program provides a vehicle for increasing the participation by DBEs in state and local procurement. DOT DBE regulations require state and local transportation agencies that receive DOT financial assistance, to establish goals for the participation of DBEs. Each DOT-assisted State and local transportation agency is required to establish annual DBE goals, and review the scopes of anticipated large prime contracts throughout the year and establish contract-specific DBE subcontracting goals. Three major DOT operating administrations are involved in the DBE program. They are the Federal Highway Administration, the Federal Aviation Administration and the Federal Transit Administration. The legal basis for the DBE program is in 46 CFR Parts 23 and 26.

The main objectives of the DBE Program are:

- To ensure that small DBEs can compete fairly for Federally funded transportation-related projects;
- To ensure that only eligible firms participate as DBEs; and
- To assist DBE firms in competing outside the DBE Program.

ELIGIBILITY

To be certified as a DBE, a firm must be a small business owned and controlled by socially and economically disadvantaged individuals. Additionally:

- An eligible DBE must be an independent business where ownership and control by a socially and economically disadvantaged individual is real, substantial and continuing. Individuals who are members of the following groups and are U.S.

citizens may be reputably presumed to be socially and economically disadvantaged: Women, Hispanic Americans, Native Americans, Asian-Pacific Americans, Subcontinent Asian Americans, African-Americans and other minorities found to be disadvantaged in the U.S. Small Business Act (15 USC 637);

- The DBE owner must share in the risks and profits of the business commensurate with his/her ownership interest and the owner must also possess the power to direct or cause the direction of the day-to-day management and major decisions of the firm; and

- There cannot be any restrictions, which prevent the DBE owner from making a business decision without the cooperation or vote of the non-DBE owner(s). If non-DBE owners of the firm are disproportionately responsible for the operation and decisions of the firm, the firm is not eligible for certification.

CERTIFICATION PROCESS

Each firm wishing to be certified as a DBE must complete and submit the DBE application and supporting documents identified on the application checklist and complete an on-site visit by the certifying agency. The certification process takes, on average, between 30- and 60-days.

Certifying agencies make the determinations based upon on-site visits, personal interviews, reviews of licenses, stock ownership, equipment, bonding capacity, work completed, résumés of principal owners and financial capacity.

CERTIFICATION APPLICATION

Download the LAUCP DBE application package at www.CertAssist.net. The DBE application is also available online at:

- WWW.LAUCP.ORG/UPC/
- WWW.NORTA.COM
- WWW.ORLEANSLEVEE.COM
- WWW.FLYMSY.COM

CONTACTS

REGION 1
LOUISIANA DEPARTMENT OF TRANSPORTATION
DOTD Compliance Programs
1201 Capitol Access Rd.
Baton Rouge, LA 70802
Phone: 225.379.1382

REGION 2
NEW ORLEANS REGIONAL TRANSIT AUTHORITY
DBE/SBE Programs
2817 Canal St.
New Orleans, LA 70119
Phone: 504.27.8408

ORLEANS LEVEE BOARD
DBE Compliance Office
6920 Franklin Ave.
New Orleans, LA 70122
Phone: 504.286.3188

LOUIS ARMSTRONG INTERNATIONAL AIRPORT
DBE Office
P.O. BOX 20007
NEW ORLEANS, LA 70141
Phone: 504.303.7611

The following list of recipients has been identified, contacted and afforded the opportunity to participate in the planning, development and implementation of Louisiana's Unified Certification Program:

1.   City of Abbeville
2.   Acadia Airport District #1 (Le Gros)
3.   Acadiana Regional Airport
4.   Airport Com. Of Airport District
5.   Alexandria International Airport
6.   City of Alexandria
7.   Allen Parish Police Jury
8.   Avoyelles Parish Police Jury
9.   Assumption Parish Police Jury
10. Baton Rouge Metro Airport
11. City of Baton Rouge – EBR Parish
12. Beauregard Parish Airport District
13. Bunkie Municipal Airport
14. Caldwell Parish Police Jury
15. Capital Area Transit System
16. Capital Region Planning Commission
17. Capital Transportation Corp.
18. Chennault International Airport
19. Claiborne Parish Police Jury

20. Concordia Parish Airport
21. Delhi Municipal Airport
22. DeSoto Parish Police Jury
23. City of DeQuincy
24. City of Donaldsonville
25. City of Eunice
26. False River Regional Airport
27. Port Fourchon
28. Town of Franklinton
29. Harry P. Williams Memorial Airport
30. Hammond Northside Regional Airport
31. City of Hammond
32. Town of Homer
33. Houma Terrebonne Airport Commission
34. Iberia Parish Government
35. IMCAL
36. Jefferson Davis Parish Police Jury
37. Jefferson Parish Transit
38. Jonesville Municipal Airport
39. Lafayette Airport Commission
40. Lafayette Parish Consolidated Govt.
41. LaSalle Parish Police Jury
42. City of Lake Charles
43. City of Leesville
44. LA DOTD
45. LA Regional Airport
46. Madison Parish Police Jury
47. Marksville Municipal Airport
48. Monroe Regional Airport
49. New Orleans Aviation Board
50. Orleans Levee District Town of Many
51. Orleans Parish Regional Planning Commission
52. City of Minden
53. City of Monroe
54. Olla Airport
55. Plaquemine Parish Government
56. Pointe Coupee Parish Police Jury
57. Town of Rayville
58. Red River Parish Police Jury
59. Regional Transit Authority
60. River Parishes Transit Authority

61. City of Ruston
62. St. Bernard Urban Rapid Transit
63. St. James Parish Council
64. St. John the Baptist Airport
65. St. Martin Parish
66. St. Mary Parish Government
67. St. Tammany Parish Government
68. St. Landry Parish Airport
69. Scott Airport
70. Shreveport Downtown Airport
71. Shreveport Regional Airport
72. City of Slidell
73. South Central Planning & Develop.
74. Southland Field
75. Springhill Airport
76. Tangipahoa Parish Council
77. Terrebonne Parish
78. Union Parish Police Jury
79. Vernon Parish Police Jury
80. Town of Vivian
81. Webster Parish Police Jury
82. West Carroll Parish Airport Authority
83. City of West Monroe
84. City of Winnfield
85. Winnsboro Municipal Airport

Visit www.CertAssist.net to access free tools, applications and information to help you navigate the business certification process. CertAssist.net has been the #1 resource on the internet for Louisiana business certification information since 2006.

LOUISIANA DEPARTMENT OF ECONOMIC DEVELOPMENT
VETERAN INITIATIVE

SUMMARY

AGENCY	**LOUISIANA DEPARTMENT OF ECONOMIC DEVELOPMENT**
DESIGNATIONS	• SERVICE-CONNECTED VETERAN OWNED • SERVICE-CONNECTED DISABLED VETERAN OWNED
RACE CONSCIOUS	NO
GENDER CONSCIOUS	NO
RECERTIFICATION	ANNUAL UPDATES
GRADUATION	NONE
FEE/COST	NONE
CERTIFICATION TIMEFRAME	48-HOURS

OVERVIEW

The Louisiana Initiative for Veteran and Service-Connected Disabled Veteran-Owned Small Entrepreneurships (the Veteran Initiative) is designed to facilitate the growth and stability of Louisiana's economy while helping veteran-owned and service-connected disabled-veteran-owned small businesses gain greater access to purchasing and contracting opportunities that are available at the state government level.

Benefits of the Veteran Initiative program include:

- Veteran Initiative firm information is accessible to state purchasing officials and prime contractors who are looking for subcontractors;
- State agencies are encouraged to get quotes from and use qualified, certified companies whenever possible;
- For purchases under $15,000.00, state agencies can waive the required additional quotes if a certified company submits a quote that is reasonable;
- 10% of the total evaluation points can be added to a bid or a request for proposal (RFP); and
- Prime contractors who use Veteran Initiative firms as subcontractors are eligible to receive additional points on their proposals.

ELIGIBILITY

A Veteran Small Entrepreneurship (VSE) is a Small Entrepreneurship (SE) that is more than 50% owned by either a Veteran, or a Disabled-in-Service Veteran. A Veteran Small Entrepreneurship (VSE) is a firm:

- Independently owned and operated;
- Not dominant in its field of operations, which shall be determined by consideration of the business' number of employees, volume of business, financial resources, competitive status, and ownership or control of materials, processes, patents, license agreements, facilities, and sales territory;

- Is owned by and has officers who are citizens or legal residents of the United States, all of whom are domiciled in Louisiana, and who maintain the principal business office in Louisiana;
- Together with its affiliate entities, has fewer than 50 full-time employees with average annual gross receipts not exceeding $5,000,000.00 per year for construction operations and $3,000,000.00 per year for non-construction operations, for each of the previous three tax years; and
- That should be able to produce a copy of a DD Form 214 and/or a U. S. Department of Veterans Affairs disability award letter if requested.

Eligibility requirements include meeting all of the criteria specified in LA. R.S. 39:2006A, as it may be amended from time to time. In order to participate and continue to participate in the program, an individual or firm must meet and continue to meet all such eligibility requirements or criteria.

CERTIFICATION PROCESS

Complete the online application at www.ledsmallbiz.com. LED will review completed applications within 48 hours of submittal. You will receive an e-mail notification after review that acknowledges your application status. Along with an acceptance notification, approved applicants will receive a certification number and instructions on how to print the Veteran Initiative certificate. You must submit annual updates through www.ledsmallbiz.com by your certification anniversary date to remain in the program.

CONTACT

John W. Matthews, Executive Director
Small Business Services
Louisiana Department of Economic Development
john.matthews@la.gov
225.342.1181

Louisiana Department of Economic Development
1051 North Third Street, Baton Rouge, LA 70802-5239
P.O. Box 94185, Baton Rouge, LA 70804-9185
800.450.8115 | 225.342.3000
www.louisianaeconomicdevelopment.com

LOUISIANA DEPARTMENT OF ECONOMIC DEVELOPMENT
SMALL & EMERGING BUSINESS DEVELOPMENT

SUMMARY

CERTIFYING AGENCY	LOUISIANA DEPARTMENT OF ECONOMIC DEVELOPMENT
DESIGNATION	SEBD
RACE CONSCIOUS	NO
GENDER CONSCIOUS	NO
RECERTIFICATION	ANNUAL UPDATES
GRADUATION	10 YEARS
FEE/COST	NONE
CERTIFICATION TIMEFRAME	72 HOURS

OVERVIEW

The Louisiana Department of Economic Development's (LED) Small and Emerging Business Development (SEBD) Program provides the managerial and technical assistance training needed to grow and sustain a small business. The SEBD program provides for developmental assistance, including entrepreneurial training, marketing, computer skills, accounting, business planning, and industry-specific assistance.

Certified SEBD firms are eligible for the Louisiana Bonding Assistance Program, are considered for bidding on select products or services purchased by state agencies and SEBD Intermediaries provide free assessments and assistance with accessing other program benefits.

ELIGIBILITY

The program is open to all Louisiana small businesses that meet the following eligibility requirements for both the business and the owner. Certification is effective for up to 10 years or until the firm no longer meets the eligibility requirements for the program.

Small and Emerging Business Person

For the purposes of the program, a person who meets all criteria in this section is defined as a Small and Emerging Business Person.

- **Citizenship** – The person is a U.S. citizen or legal resident
- **Louisiana Residency** – The person has been a Louisiana resident for at least one year
- **Net Worth** – At least 51% of the business is owned and controlled by persons who individually have a net worth of less than $400,000.00, excluding personal residence, business assets and retirement accounts
- **Full-Time Employment** – Managing owners who claim Small and Emerging Business Person status must be full-time employees of the applicant firm (20 or more hours per week)

Small and Emerging Business

A business that meets all criteria below is defined as a Small and Emerging Business for this program:

- **Ownership and Control** – At least 51% of the company is owned and controlled by one or more Small and Emerging Business Persons
- **Principal Place of Business** – The firm's principal place of business is Louisiana
- **Lawful Function** – The company has been organized for profit to perform a commercially useful function
- **Business Net Worth** – The business' net worth does not exceed $1.5 million
- **Job Creation** – An applicant firm anticipates creating new full-time jobs

CERTIFICATION PROCESS

Complete the online application at www.ledsmallbiz.com. LED will review completed applications within 72 hours of submittal. You will receive an e-mail notification after review that acknowledges your application status. Along with an acceptance notification, approved applicants will receive a certification number, a list of SEBD Intermediaries, and instructions on how to print the SEBD certificate. You must submit annual updates through www.ledsmallbiz.com by your certification anniversary date to remain in the program.

CONTACT

John W. Matthews, Executive Director
Small Business Services
Louisiana Department of Economic Development
john.matthews@la.gov
225.342.1181

Louisiana Department of Economic Development
1051 North Third Street, Baton Rouge, LA 70802-5239
P.O. Box 94185, Baton Rouge, LA 70804-9185
800.450.8115 | 225.342.3000
www.louisianaeconomicdevelopment.com

LOUISIANA DEPARTMENT OF ECONOMIC DEVELOPMENT
HUDSON INITIATVE

SUMMARY

CERTIFYING AGENCY	**LOUISIANA DEPARTMENT OF ECONOMIC DEVELOPMENT**
DESIGNATION	HUDSON INITIATIVE
RACE CONSCIOUS	NO
GENDER CONSCIOUS	NO
RECERTIFICATION	ANNUAL UPDATES
GRADUATION	NONE
FEE/COST	NONE
CERTIFICATION TIMEFRAME	48 HOURS

OVERVIEW

Louisiana's Hudson Initiative is a certification program designed to help eligible Louisiana small businesses gain greater access to purchasing and contracting opportunities that are available at the State government level. Through the Hudson Initiative:

- Your business and contact information will be accessible to State purchasing officials and prime contractors looking for subcontractors;
- State agencies are encouraged to get quotes from and use qualified, certified companies whenever possible;
- For small purchases of less than $15,000.00, State agencies can waive the requirement of getting additional quotes if a certified company submits a quote that is reasonable;
- 10% of the total evaluation points can be added to your bid on a Request for Proposal (RFP); and
- Prime contractors who use your business as a subcontractor on a bid for an RFP are also eligible to receive additional percentage points on their bid.

ELIGIBILITY

The program is open to all Louisiana businesses that meet the following eligibility requirements of a Small Entrepreneurship (SE) under the Hudson Initiative:

- **Principal Place of Business** – The company must have its principal place of business in Louisiana
- **Employees** – The company has fewer than 50 full-time employees
- **Average Annual Gross Receipts** – Average annual gross receipts do not exceed $5 million for non-construction and $10 million for construction companies
- **Independently Owned and Operated** – The business is independently owned and operated
- **Not Dominant** – The business is not dominant in its professional field
- **Louisiana Residency** – Owned by persons domiciled in Louisiana
- **Citizenship** – Owned by and has officers who are U.S. citizens or legal residents

CERTIFICATION PROCESS

Complete the online application at www.ledsmallbiz.com. LED will review completed applications within two business days of submittal. You will receive an e-mail notification after review that acknowledges your application status. You must submit annual updates through www.ledsmallbiz.com by your certification anniversary date to remain in the program.

CONTACT

John W. Matthews, Executive Director
Small Business Services
Louisiana Department of Economic Development
john.matthews@la.gov
225.342.1181

Louisiana Department of Economic Development
1051 North Third Street, Baton Rouge, LA 70802-5239
P.O. Box 94185, Baton Rouge, LA 70804-9185
800.450.8115 | 225.342.3000
www.louisianaeconomicdevelopment.com

CITY OF NEW ORLEANS
STATE & LOCAL DISADVANTAGED BUSINESS ENTERPRISE

SUMMARY

CERTIFYING AGENCIES	CITY OF NEW ORLEANS SEWERAGE & WATER BOARD OF NEW ORLEANS NEW ORLEANS AVIATION BOARD HARRAH'S CASINO NEW ORLEANS (HEREINAFTER REFERRED TO AS 'SLDBE PARTNER AGENCIES')
DESIGNATION	SLDBE
RACE CONSCIOUS	NO
GENDER CONSCIOUS	NO
RECERTIFICATION	BI-ANNUAL
GRADUATION	NONE
FEE/COST	NONE
CERTIFICATION TIMEFRAME	7-10 DAYS (Improved timeframe beginning in 2016)

OVERVIEW

SLDBE Partner Agencies operate the State and Local Disadvantaged Business Enterprise Program (hereinafter referred to as the 'SLDBE Program' or 'the Program'). The program is a race and gender neutral disadvantaged business enterprise (DBE) program that provides for the participation of businesses owned by socially and economically disadvantaged persons to increase their participation in contracting opportunities with the SLDBE partner agencies.

In 2003, the City of New Orleans joined with the Sewerage & Water Board of New Orleans (SWB) and the New Orleans Aviation Board (NOAB) in a cooperative agreement to operate the SLDBE Program. Harrah's Casino New Orleans became a partner agency in 2009. Approval for the SLDBE program through any of the partner agencies qualifies a firm to bid and perform as an SLDBE firm with any of the partner agencies.

ELIGIBILITY

The SLDBE Program is a race and gender-neutral program that does not presume social and economic disadvantage. A business may qualify for the SLDBE Program if:

- It is determined that the business' ability to compete in the business world has been restricted due to industry practices, limited access to capital, and/or restricted credit opportunities that are beyond their control;
- The business is owned, operated and controlled by one or more socially and economically disadvantaged person(s) and that person or those persons own, operate, and control at least 51% of the company;
- The firm is an independent business (not a franchise) in which the ownership and control by a socially and economically disadvantaged person is real, substantial and continuing;

- The SLDBE owners share in the risks and profits commensurate with their ownership interests;
- The SLDBE owners possess the power to direct or cause the direction of day-to-day management and major decisions of the firm; and
- There can be no restrictions in the bylaws, operating agreement, or other document, that prevents the SLDBE owner(s) from making a business decision without the corporation or vote of the non-SLDBE owner(s).

CERTIFICATION PROCESS

Each firm wishing to be certified as a SLDBE must complete and submit the SLDBE application and supporting documents identified on the application checklist and complete an on-site visit. The certification process takes, on average, between 7- and 10- business days.

Any firm which believes that it has been wrongly denied certification as a SLDBE firm may file an appeal with the Certification Panel for a review of the denial and present information and writing to the Certification Panel. The appeal must filed no later than ten (10) days after the date of the letter of notification certification denial.

The SLDBE certification application is available at www.CertAssist.net and at:

- www.nola.gov
- www.flymsy.com
- www.swbno.org

CONTACTS

CITY OF NEW ORLEANS
OFFICE OF SUPPLIER DIVERSITY
1100 POYDRAS ST., SUITE 1800
NEW ORLEANS, LA 70112
504.658.4200
WWW.NOLA.GOV

SEWERAGE & WATER BOARD OF NEW ORLEANS
ECONOMICALLY DISADVANTAGED
BUSINESS OFFICE
625 ST. JOSEPH ST., ROOM 305
NEW ORLEANS, LA 70165
504.582.6112
WWW.SWBNO.ORG

NEW ORLEANS AVIATION BOARD
DISADVANTAGED BUSINESS
ENTERPRISE OFFICE
P.O. BOX 20007
NEW ORLEANS, LA 70141
504.303.7611
WWW.FLYMSY.COM

HARRAH'S CASINO NEW ORLEANS
SUPPLIER DIVERSITY/DBE PROGRAM
504.533.6000|504.533.6159
WWW.HARRAHSNEWORLEANS.COM

NEW ORLEANS REGIONAL TRANSIT AUTHORITY
SMALL BUSINESS ENTERPRISE

SUMMARY

CERTIFYING AGENCY	**NEW ORLEANS REGIONAL TRANSIT AUTHORITY**
DESIGNATION	SBE
RACE CONSCIOUS	NO
GENDER CONSCIOUS	NO
RECERTIFICATION	ANNUAL
GRADUATION	WHEN THE FIRM NO LONGER MEETS THE SBA SIZE STANDARD IN ITS PRIMARY NAICS CODE
FEE/COST	NONE
CERTIFICATION TIMEFRAME	30-60 DAYS

OVERVIEW

The New Orleans Regional Transit Authority's (NORTA's) Small Business Enterprise (SBE) Program is open to all business owners regardless of race, ethnicity or gender. The SBE Program is used for both federally and non-Federally funded procurement projects at NORTA. As such, once a business is certified as an SBE the firm can bid and perform as an SBE on any NORTA project. Businesses that are currently Disadvantaged Business Enterprise (DBE) certified with the Louisiana Unified Certification Program (LAUCP) must submit an SBE Affidavit of Certification Eligibility. The LAUCP DBE certification will automatically certify a business as an eligible SBE with NORTA. Businesses that are owned by minorities or women, that are not currently LAUCP DBE certified, must submit a complete SBE certification application to NORTA

ELIGIBILITY

To be an eligible Small Business Enterprise a business must be for-profit and must meet the annual gross receipts cap as defined in 49 CFR Part 26 [Average annual gross receipts, as defined by SBA regulations (see 13 CFR 121.402), over the firm's previous three fiscal years, in excess of $22.41 million]. The business must also meet the SBA industry size standard defined by the Small Business Administration.

The business must have a least 51% ownership by a person who is economically disadvantaged. To be considered economically disadvantaged the individual's Personal Net Worth, not including their primary place of residence or ownership in the business, cannot exceed $1.32 million in compliance with the 49 CFR Part 26.67. An SBE business owner must be a U.S. Citizen or lawfully permanent resident of the U.S.

CERTIFICATION PROCESS

The SBE application is available online at http://www.norta.com/Business_Center and www.CertAssist.net. Complete and submit the certification application, along with the supporting documents, to NORTA's Director of Small Business Development. The small business development team will review the application package for completeness and will schedule and conduct an on-site visit of your business. The certification process typically takes between 30-60 days.

CONTACTS

Small Business Enterprise Program
Judith Dangerfield, Director
Office of Small Business Development
Veolia Transportation in Service to the RTA
2817 Canal St.
New Orleans, LA 70119
Phone: 504.827.8408

LAUCP DBE Program
Janice Abide, Title VI Coordinator
Veolia Transportation in Service to the RTA
2817 Canal St.
New Orleans, LA 70119
Phone: 504.827.8308

RECOVERY SCHOOL DISTRCT OF NEW ORLEANS
DISADVANTAGED BUSINESS ENTERPRISE REGISTRATION

SUMMARY

AGENCY	**RECOVERY SCHOOL DISTRICT OF NEW ORLEANS**
DESIGNATION	REGISTERED DBE
RACE CONSCIOUS	NO
GENDER CONSCIOUS	NO
RECERTIFICATION	DEPENDENT ON CERTIFYING AGENCY
GRADUATION	DEPENDENT ON CERTIFYING AGENCY
FEE/COST	NONE
CERTIFICATION TIMEFRAME	UP TO 10-BUSINESS DAYS

OVERVIEW

The Recovery School District of New Orleans (RSD) has established the DBE Office to encourage the participation of certified DBE firms in planning, building and renovating schools throughout the city. The RSD does not have an independent DBE certification process, but it does have a DBE program and DBE Office. The DBE Office:

- Provides 'entrance points' for and information to qualified DBEs seeking participation in RSD construction projects;
- Keeps general contractors informed of interested, qualified DBEs and DBE outreach opportunities/mechanisms;
- Keeps interested, qualified DBEs informed of RSD opportunities and events;
- Engages RSD contractors, providing assistance in addressing barriers to meeting compliance goals and with identifying/articulating 'good faith' efforts; and
- Tracks, reviews and reports contractor compliance.

ELIGIBILITY

A business must be certified through the Louisiana Unified Certification Program as a DBE or through the City of New Orleans, Sewerage and Water Board of New Orleans, New Orleans Aviation Board or Harrah's Casino as a SLDBE to qualify as a DBE for the RSD.

REGISTRATION PROCESS

Download and complete the RSD's **DBE Vendor Information Sheet** and submit it along with proof of DBE certification to the RSD DBE Office. The application is available at www.CertAssist.net and at www.rsdla.net.

CONTACT

Sombra Williams, Director
Disadvantaged Business Enterprise Program
Recovery School District of New Orleans
504.373.6200 ext. 20082
dbe@rsdla.net

Ensure that any transfer of ownership, stocks/shares, or control of the applicant firm does not coincide with the submission of an application for DBE certification.

HOUSING AUTHORITY OF NEW ORLEANS DISADVANTAGED BUSINESS ENTERPRISE & WOMEN-OWNED BUSINESS ENTERPRISE

SUMMARY

CERTTIFYING AGENCY	HOUSING AUTHORITY OF NEW ORLEANS
DESIGNATIONS	DBE WBE
RACE CONSCIOUS	NO
GENDER CONSCIOUS	DBE (NO)/WBE (YES)
RECERTIFICATION	ANNUAL
GRADUATION	NONE
FEE/COST	NONE
CERTIFICATION TIMEFRAME	10-BUSINESS DAYS

OVERVIEW

HANO does not have an independent DBE/WBE certification process. HANO grants full certification up to one (1) year upon receipt of written letter from one of the Louisiana Unified Certification Program (LAUCP) certifying agencies that a company is a LAUCP certified DBE or WBE. Annual verification is required by the vendor to show proof of continued certification through the Louisiana Unified Certification Program.

ELIGIBILITY

All firms certified as DBE or WBE through the LAUCP.

CERTIFICATION PROCESS

Download and complete HANO's **DBE Program Certification Application** and submit it along with proof of DBE/WBE certification to the HANO's Section 3/DBE/WBE Office. The application is available www.CertAssist.net and at www.hano.org.

CONTACT

Larry Barabino, Jr.
Section 3/DBE/WBE Coordinator
Housing Authority of New Orleans
4100 Touro Street
New Orleans, LA 70122
Office: 504.670.3268
Fax: 504.286.1422
lbarabino@hano.org

Most programs classify certified firms by NAICS Codes, SIC Codes, CSI Codes, or NIGP Codes. Make sure your firm's "Codes" align with your core competencies to improve your potential contracting opportunities.

HOUSING AUTHORITY OF NEW ORLEANS
HUD SECTION 3 BUSINESS

SUMMARY

CERTTIFYING AGENCY	HOUSING AUTHORITY OF NEW ORLEANS
DESIGNATION	SECTION 3 BUSINESS
RACE CONSCIOUS	NO
GENDER CONSCIOUS	NO
RECERTIFICATION	ANNUAL UPDATES
GRADUATION	NONE
FEE/COST	NONE
CERTIFICATION TIMEFRAME	10-BUSINESS DAYS

OVERVIEW

Section 3 is a provision of the Housing and Urban Development (HUD) Act of 1968 that helps foster local economic development, neighborhood economic improvement, and individual self-sufficiency. The Section 3 program requires that recipients of certain HUD financial assistance, to the greatest extent feasible, provide job training, employment and contracting opportunities for low- or very-low income residents in connection with projects and activities in their neighborhoods. Income limits for Orleans Parish appear on the following page.

In order to meet the requirements of the Section 3 provision, the Housing Authority of New Orleans (HANO) grants full certification up to one (1) year to Orleans Parish businesses that meet Section 3 business certification eligibility.

ELIGIBILITY

Those businesses that qualify to receive a Section 3 Business Certification include:

1. Business concerns that are 51% or more owned and controlled by residents of any HANO housing site or whose full-time permanent workforce includes 30% of HANO residents of any housing site; or
2. HUD Youthbuild programs in Orleans Parish; or
3. Business concerns that are 51% or more owned and controlled by HANO residents or are low or very low-income Orleans Parish residents or whose full-time permanent work force includes 30% HANO residents or low/very low-income Orleans Parish residents; and
4. Businesses that subcontract in excess of 25% of the total amount of subcontracts to business concerns identified in the preferences above.

CERTIFICATION PROCESS

Download and complete **SECTION 5** of HANO's DBE Program Certification Application. Submit the application and supporting documents to HANO's Section 3/DBE/WBE Office. The application is available at www.CertAssist.net and at www.hano.org.

CONTACT
Larry Barabino, Jr.
Section 3/DBE/WBE Coordinator
Housing Authority of New Orleans
4100 Touro Street
New Orleans, LA 70122
Office: 504.670.3268
Fax: 504.286.1422
lbarabino@hano.org

Note:
Orleans Parish is part of the New Orleans-Metairie-Kenner, LA Metropolitan Statistical Area (MSA). All information presented in the table above applies to Jefferson Parish, Orleans Parish, Plaquemines Parish, St. Bernard Parish, St. Charles Parish, St. John the Baptist Parish and St. Tammany Parish.

Current HUD Income Limits can be found at **www.hud.gov**

ORLEANS PARISH SCHOOL BOARD
DISADVANTAGED BUSINESS ENTERPRISE

SUMMARY

AGENCY	**RECOVERY SCHOOL DISTRICT OF NEW ORLEANS**
DESIGNATION	REGISTERED DBE
RACE CONSCIOUS	NO
GENDER CONSCIOUS	NO
RECERTIFICATION	DEPENDENT ON CERTIFYING AGENCY
GRADUATION	DEPENDENT ON CERTIFYING AGENCY
FEE/COST	NONE
CERTIFICATION TIMEFRAME	N/A

OVERVIEW

The Orleans Parish School Board (OPSB) has established the DBE Office to encourage the participation of certified DBE firms in procurement opportunities with OPSB. OPSB does not have an independent DBE certification process, but it does accept DBE certifications from the City of New Orleans (SLDBE) and Louisiana Unified Certification Program (LAUCP).

OPSB's DBE Office:

- Maintains 'entrance points' for qualified DBEs seeking participation in OPSB construction projects;
- Keeps general contractors informed of interested, qualified DBEs and DBE outreach opportunities/mechanisms;
- Keeps interested, qualified DBEs informed of OPSB opportunities and events;
- Engages OPSB contractors, providing assistance in addressing barriers to meeting compliance goals and with identifying/articulating 'good faith' efforts; and
- Tracks, reviews and reports contractor compliance.

ELIGIBILITY

A business must be certified as a DBE through the LAUCP or as a SLDBE or through the City of New Orleans, Sewerage and Water Board of New Orleans, New Orleans Aviation Board or Harrah's Casino.

REGISTRATION PROCESS

There is no registration requirement at this time. Proof of certification is required for participation on an OPSB project as a DBE.

CONTACT

DBE Program
Orleans Parish School Board
504.304.5584

Keep a copy of your certification application
package on file in case you need to refer to it
during the on-site visit or if you need it in
preparation for your firm's recertification.

CITY/PARISH OF BATON ROUGE
SMALL BUSINESS ENTERPRISE

SUMMARY

AGENCY	CITY/PARISH OF BATON ROUGE
DESIGNATION	SBE
RACE CONSCIOUS	NO
GENDER CONSCIOUS	NO
RECERTIFICATION	ANNUAL
GRADUATION	NONE
FEE/COST	NONE
CERTIFICATION TIMEFRAME	30-60 DAYS

OVERVIEW

The City/Parish of East Baton Rouge has established the Small Business Enterprise (SBE) program to grow small businesses and to help prepare them to become more competitive when competing for City-Parish contracts. The SBE program provides several benefits to small businesses:

- You will receive notices of formal and informal City/Parish contracting opportunities available for bid;
- Your company will be included in the city-wide SBE database;
- You will be invited to attend our *Business with the Baton Rouge* networking sessions; and
- You can attend exclusive business training programs such as Contractor's College® and NXTLevel®.

ELIGIBILITY

- A business that is licensed and for-profit and performs a legal, commercially useful function;
- A business that does not exceed the small business size standards as established by the U.S. Small Business Administration for the firm's primary NAICS code;
- A business that has been actively in business for at least one year;
- A business with 51% or more of the ownership in the business is by a socially and economically disadvantaged owner. A socially and economically disadvantage owner is one who has a personal net worth under $1,320,000.00 (exclusions apply. See the SBE application for details).

CERTIFICATION PROCESS

- Download the SBE application from www.CertAssist.net or www.brgov.com/dept/mayor/bbr/sbe.htm;
- Download and complete the Personal Net Worth Statement;
- Sign and notarize the DBE/SBE Affidavit and hand deliver or mail the required documents for approval.

- Current LAUCP Certified DBE's may become a SBE by submitting a copy of their DBE certification letter and notarizing the DBE/SBE Affidavit.

CONTACT
Business Development Coordinator
City/Parish of Baton Rouge
300 Louisiana Ave., 2nd Floor • Baton Rouge, LA 70806
225.389.3039

Note: *Final program authorization and approval is pending as of the publication of this guidebook. Contact the City/Parish of Baton Rouge for the latest program updates.*

EAST BATON ROUGE PARISH PUBLIC SCHOOL SYSTEM
FAIR SHARE PROGRAM

SUMMARY

CERTIFYING AGENCY	EAST BATON ROUGE PARISH SCHOOL SYSTEM
DESIGNATIONS	MBE WBE DBE
RACE CONSCIOUS	YES (For MBE designation ONLY)
GENDER CONSCIOUS	YES (For WBE designation ONLY)
RECERTIFICATION	ANNUAL
GRADUATION	NONE
FEE/COST	NONE
CERTIFICATION TIMEFRAME	15-30 BUSINESS DAYS

OVERVIEW

East Baton Rouge Parish School System (EBRPSS) adopted the **EBRPSS Fair Share Program** ("Program") in July 2009 and the Minority and Women Business Enterprise Procurement Policy in July 2011.

Policy

It is the policy of the EBRPSS to provide equal opportunities to all contractors and bidders. The EBRPSS specifically encourages Minority and Women Owned Business Enterprises (M/W/DBEs) to fully participate in all phases of its procurement and contracting opportunities and to afford them a full and fair opportunity to compete for District contracts. The Board establishes an annual goal of at least twenty (20%) percent for M/W/DBE participation in contract and procurement opportunities.

*The Board also encourages M/WBEs to acquire Disadvantaged Business Enterprise (DBE) certification through one of the certifying agencies provided for in the Louisiana Unified Certified Program for Disadvantaged Business Enterprises. **DBE certification is preferred and strongly encouraged.***

The Superintendent of Schools shall provide a quarterly report to the Board as to the effectiveness of reaching and maintaining the annual goal. The Superintendent of Schools shall require that all contracts and purchases require contractors and vendors to maintain Equal Employment Opportunity Policies.

The program seeks to enforce the EBRPSS's policy of providing and ensuring contracting and procurement opportunities for M/W/DBEs and to level the playing field for M/W/DBEs that wish to do business with the EBRPSS.

Program managers for EBRPSS, CSRS and Aramark, along with EBRPSS departments and individual schools are all charged with complying with the Program to ensure contracting and procurement opportunities for M/W/DBEs.

PROGRAM GOALS

- Twenty percent (20%) utilization of minority, women and disadvantaged business enterprises (M/W/DBEs) in the procurement of goods and services[1] by EBRPSS;
- Provide optimum customer service to M/W/DBEs; and
- Create key partnerships in the local community and throughout Louisiana.

ELIGIBILITY

- The firm must be an independent business, organized for profit, and legally licensed to do business in Louisiana that is owned by a U.S. citizen or lawful permanent resident who is a member of one of the following groups:
  Women or ethnic minority: Black/African-American, Hispanic-/Latin-American, American Indian/Alaskan Native, Asian American or Pacific Islander
- The eligible owner(s) must own at least 51% of the business;
- The eligible owner must control the firm's day-to-day operations;
- The eligible owner must have both the legal authority and technical ability to control the firm. If the state of Louisiana requires a professional license to perform the firm's line of work, the eligible owner must hold this license, even if the owner is not the one performing the work.
- Out of state firms that do not have a physical office location in Louisiana may be required to have a Louisiana Business License in order to participate as an eligible firm.

CERTIFICATION PROCESS

Application(s) are available at http://www.ebrschools.org/explore.cfm/fairshareprogram/

1. Download and complete the **EBRPSS Fair Share Application.**
2. If your firm is a certified DBE through the Louisiana Department of Transportation, download and complete the **EBRPSS Fair Share Application for (LAUCP) DBEs.**
3. ALL applicants must complete the **EBRPSS Vendor Form.**
4. Return the application and required documents to the address below for review and approval.

CONTACT

Fair Share Program
East Baton Rouge Parish Schools
2875 Michelli Drive
Baton Rouge, LA 70805
Phone: 225-226-3725
FAX: 225-226-3713

---

[1] Goods and services include, but are not limited to, professional services, materials, and supplies.

CITY OF SHREVEPORT
FAIR SHARE PROGRAM

SUMMARY

CERTIFYING AGENCY	**CITY OF SHREVEPORT**
DESIGNATION	REGISTERED FAIR SHARE PROGRAM BUSINESS
RACE CONSCIOUS	NO
GENDER CONSCIOUS	NO
RECERTIFICATION	NONE
GRADUATION	NONE
FEE/COST	NONE
CERTIFICATION TIMEFRAME	30-60 BUSINESS DAYS

OVERVIEW

The City of Shreveport's Fair Share Initiative was originated by Ordinance on July 27, 1999. The overall intent of the Ordinance and resulting plan was to develop an office dedicated to serving the needs of small economically disadvantage businesses. Implementation of the program began on January 1, 2000.

The Fair Share Program seeks to enforce the City's policy of providing and ensuring contracting and procurement opportunities for small economically disadvantaged businesses. Additionally, The Fair Share Ordinance is a concept unique to the City of Shreveport in its effort to bring more DBEs into the economic mainstream of the local economy. Simply put, the program aims to "level the economic playing field." The major intent of the program is to provide opportunities for companies and individuals to do business with the City of Shreveport where opportunities may not have existed in the past.

ELIGIBILITY

A small economically disadvantaged business is a firm that is owned and controlled by one or more economically disadvantaged individuals and meets the requirements of small disadvantaged businesses. Eligibility requirements fall into two categories that apply to the individual owners and to the applicant firm. In order to continue participation in the Fair Share Program, a firm and its individual owners must continue to meet all eligibility requirements.

A. Economically Disadvantaged Persons

Under the Fair Share Program, a person who meets all of the criteria in this section shall be defined as an Economically Disadvantaged Individual.

1. Citizenship - the person is a citizen or lawful permanent resident of the U.S.
2. Net Worth - each individual owner's personal net worth may not exceed $250,000. The value of an individual's personal residence and his/her investment in the applicant firm will be excluded when calculating individual net worth for the Program.

3. Income - each individual owner must submit personal Federal Income Tax Returns for the past three years.

B. **Economically Disadvantaged Business**
   1. Ownership and Control - At least 51% of the company must be owned and controlled by one or more economically disadvantaged individuals.
   2. Business Size – Under the Fair Share Program, an eligible firm's size shall be defined as 50% or less of the published U. S. Small Business Administration's (SBA) size standards by SIC or NAIC codes.
   3. Lawful Function - The company is organized for profit to perform a lawful, commercially useful function.
   4. Business Net Worth - The company's net worth at the time of application may not exceed $750,000. The DBE Office may waive this requirement only in those instances where the business seeking certification is in a capital-intensive business.
   5. Diminished Capital and Credit - A firm will be considered to have diminished capital and credit if its ability to compete in the free enterprise system has been impaired due to diminished capital and credit opportunities as compared to other firms in the same or similar line of business and whose diminished opportunities have precluded, or are likely to preclude, such firm from successfully competing in the open market. Examples of diminished capital and credit are lack of access to long-term financing or credit, working capital financing, equipment trade credit, raw materials, supplier trade credit and bonding. The applicant must furnish documentation that credit has previously been denied for an area of credit that applies to the firm's type of business, condition or situation. Applicant firms that score poorly on all financial measures published by the Risk Management Association (www.rmahq.org) for liquidity, leverage, operating efficiency and profitability, and considered economically disadvantaged.

      Factors for consideration include, but are not limited to:
      a) Business assets
      b) Net worth
      c) Income
      d) Profit

   6. Full Time - Managing owners who claim economically disadvantaged status must be full time employees of the applicant firm.

C. **Documents Required for Certification**
The application shall be supported by, but not limited to, the following documents:

   1. Business's balance sheet and income statement
   2. Verification of signatories on bank accounts

3. Copies of income tax returns
4. Résumés of owner and top managers
5. Copies of business licenses and permits
6. Copies of stock certificates, stock transfer ledgers, and Articles of Incorporation for corporations or copies of membership certificates, membership transfer ledgers and Articles of Organization for limited liability companies

CERTIFICATION PROCESS

1. Download the application package from www.CertAssist.net or www.shreveportla.gov.
2. Complete the Fair Share Program Certification Affidavit, Vendor Application and an IRS Form W-9.
3. Return the documents to the address below.
4. Your package will be reviewed and a site visit of your place of business will be scheduled.
5. An award Letter of Certification will be issued to you.

CONTACT

City of Shreveport Fair Share Plan
P.O. Box 31109
Shreveport, LA 71130
Office: 318.673.5060

Create 'TABS' or cover sheets to organize your supporting documents behind your certification application. If a supporting document is not relevant to your business, write "N/A" or explain why it is not in a short statement. If you do not write a response, it may be interpreted as if you left the supporting document out of your application package, making application package appear incomplete.

CITY OF SHREVEPORT
DISADVANTAGE BUSINESS ENTERPRISE

SUMMARY

CERTIFYING AGENCY	CITY OF SHREVEPORT
DESIGNATION	DBE
RACE CONSCIOUS	NO
GENDER CONSCIOUS	NO
RECERTIFICATION	ANNUAL
GRADUATION	NONE
FEE/COST	NONE
CERTIFICATION TIMEFRAME	30-90 DAYS

OVERVIEW

The Disadvantaged Business Enterprise (DBE) program handles certification for all socially and economically disadvantaged businesses for all departments of the City of Shreveport and other local public entities having that need. The office is also the certifying agent for the North Louisiana Purchasing Network, a volunteer organization of local large corporations committed to improving relationships between these companies and area DBE businesses.

The DBE office provides disadvantaged businesses the opportunities to diversify and grow through various services and referrals. As part of the Department of Community Development, the DBE Program has been mandated by the Department to perform and monitor identified functions that will enhance the City's DBE economic participation. In addition to City mandates, the DBE program employs the requirements and measurements as outlined in the Federal regulations relative to funding sources received by the City.

ELIGIBILITY

Businesses organized for profit and performing a commercially useful function are eligible for certification. The business must be at least 51% owned, controlled and actively operated by persons determined to be disadvantaged.

CERTIFICATION PROCESS

1. Download the application at www.CertAssist.net or http://www.shreveportla.gov.
2. The completed application, along with supporting documentation, must be brought IN PERSON to the DBE Office, City Hall Annex, 1237 Murphy Street, Room 210, Shreveport, Louisiana 71101.
3. Consultation with the applicant is done to ensure the applicant understands the requirements of the application and questions are answered or researched for the applicant.

4. The application is reviewed to check for the authenticity of the document. If there are any incomplete blocks, the applicant is asked to forward the necessary information.
5. Upon completion of the review, a site visit is scheduled with the applicant. The site visit is conducted to verify the information listed by the applicant. A site visit is conducted upon initial certification and for recertification, if required.
6. A letter awarding certification is provided to the applicant along with a certificate with the Community Service Bureau Chief's signature. The dates of certification and expiration appear on the certificate.

CONTACTS
City of Shreveport DBE office
City Hall Annex
1237 Murphy Street, Room 210
Shreveport, LA 71101
Office: 318.673.7566

SOUTHERN REGIONAL
MINORITY SUPPLIER DEVELOPMENT COUNCIL
MINORITY BUSINESS ENTERPRISE

SUMMARY

CERTTIFYING AGENCY	**SOUTHERN REGIONAL MINORITY SUPPLIER DEVELOPMENT COUNCIL**
DESIGNATION	MBE
RACE CONSCIOUS	YES (ETHNIC MINORITIES ONLY)
GENDER CONSCIOUS	NO
RECERTIFICATION	ANNUAL
GRADUATION	NONE
FEES/COST	$300.00-$700.00 (CERTIFICATION) $200.00-$650.00 (ANNUAL RE-CERTIFICATION)
CERTIFICATION TIMEFRAME	30-60 DAYS

OVERVIEW

Certification with the Southern Regional Minority Supplier Development Council (SRMSDC) provides minority-owned businesses with valuable resources to help them grow and succeed. SRMSDC offers minority-owned businesses an excellent opportunity to meet with corporate buyers who are interested in working with qualified and certified minority business enterprises (MBEs).

SRMSDC offers formal and informal venues to meet with corporate buyers so MBEs can learn about national, state and local opportunities and expand professional networks. SRMSDC is an affiliate of the National Minority Supplier Development Council (NMSDC), the largest national organization whose certification is recognized uniformly by corporate America.

Benefits of MBE certification:

- More than two-thirds of MBEs confirm an increase in revenues as a result of partnership with corporate members of the NMSDC
- MBEs gain access to over 3,500 leading global, national, regional and local companies and their buyers
- MBEs are listed in the regional and national certified MBE database
- MBEs have the ability to participation in education programs and workshops to assist in personal, financial and professional growth
- MBEs have the opportunity to network with corporate members, MBEs and business owners at SRMSDC events and activities
- MBEs gain access to second tier and MBE to MBE business opportunities

ELIGIBILITY

To become a certified MBE, a business must meet the following requirements. Both current and historical facts are considered in determining ownership qualifications and participation in the management and operations of the company.

- The business is a for-profit enterprise organized for a legal purpose
- The business is physically located in the United States of or one of its trust territories
- The business is at least 51% ethnic minority owned:
  Ethnic minority owned is defined as any business having owner(s) belonging to the following minority groups: African-American, Hispanic-American, Native American, Asian and Pacific Islander American (Asian-Indian included)
- The ethnic minority owner must be a U.S. citizen and must be active in the day-to-day operations of the business

CERTIFICATION PROCESS

1. Register as a user online at WWW.SRMSDC.ORG.
2. **Complete the online Certification application.** Certification starts with the online application. You may take as long as necessary to complete the application. Your information will be saved for your next session and is completely confidential.
3. **Pay the application fee.** You may pay by credit card or send a check. Your application will be processed after payment is received.
4. **Send or hand deliver the required supporting documentation (Page 3) to SRMSDC's office.** SRMSDCC requires specific documents to complete the Certification process. The documentation must be sent through postal mail. Upon receipt, the application and supporting documents are reviewed for completeness.
5. **Site Visit.** SRMSDC will perform a site visit of your business office and conduct a personal interview of the owner(s).
6. **Committee Review.** The Certification Committee will review your application for MBE certification and must approve the application before it can be submitted to the Board for final approval.
7. **Board Review.** The Board will review the Certification Committee's recommendation and make the final decision. If the Board rejects the application, you may submit a letter of appeal. If approved, you will be notified by e-mail and postal mail.

CONTACT

MBE Certification
Louisiana Minority Supplier Development Council
400 Poydras St., Suite 1960
New Orleans, LA 70122
Office: 504.293.0400

WOMEN'S BUSINESS ENTERPRISE NATIONAL COUNCIL-SOUTH
WOMEN-OWNED BUSINESS ENTERPRISE

SUMMARY

CERTTIFYING AGENCY	**WOMEN'S BUSINESS ENTERPRISE NATIONAL COUNCIL- SOUTH**
DESIGNATION	WBE
RACE CONSCIOUS	NO
GENDER CONSCIOUS	YES (WOMEN ONLY)
RECERTIFICATION	ANNUAL
GRADUATION	NONE
FEES	$350.00 TO $1,000.00 (BASED ON ANNUAL REVENUES) [FEES ARE THE SAME FOR RE-CERTIFICATION]
CERTIFICATION TIMEFRAME	30-60 DAYS

OVERVIEW

Women's Business Enterprise Council South (WBEC South) works with the Women's Business Enterprise National Council (WBENC) to connect WBENC-Certified Women's Business Enterprises (WBEs) with WBENC's Corporate Members and WBEC South's Corporate Partners to facilitate real time business opportunities at the local level.

WBENC is also an approved Third Party Certifier for the United States Small Business Administration's (SBA) Women-Owned Small Business (WOSB) Federal Contracting Program. This designation gives WBEC South the accreditation needed to process WBE WOSB applications. WBEC South does not charge a fee to WBENC Certified WBEs that qualify for the WOSB Certification. You must be a current WBENC Certified WBE in order to have your WOSB application processed by WBEC South.

Benefits of WBE certification:

- Get noticed by thousands of major U.S. corporations and several public agencies
- Gain exposure by exhibiting at WBENC's national business conference, attended each year by hundreds of corporate supplier diversity professionals
- Be included in an online database used by corporate members and other certified women-owned businesses across the country to find talented suppliers
- Meet, mingle, commiserate and do business with other talented professional women business owners
- Identify new targets with access to a current list of supplier diversity and procurement executives at thousands of major U.S. corporations
- Strengthen marketing efforts by featuring the WBENC member seal on company promotional materials
- Receive regular e-mails highlighting new sourcing opportunities from WBENC
- Compete to receive a Dorothy B. Brothers Scholarship to continue your executive management education

- Participate in the Tuck-WBENC Executive Program, a five-day executive development program to help you grow and expand your business

ELIGIBILITY

- The applicant company must be "small" in its primary industry in accordance with SBA's size standards for that industry;
- The applicant company must be at least fifty-one percent (51%) unconditionally and directly owned and controlled by one or more women who are U.S. citizens;
- Management and daily operation must be controlled by one or more of the women owners;
- The women owners must make long-term decisions for the business; and
- One of the criteria below must also be true for CORPORATIONS ONLY:

  - Women must make up a majority of the Board of Directors or have a majority of the Board votes through weighted voting
  - Women must make up 51% of the voting power, sit on the Board AND have enough voting power to overcome any supermajority requirement

Firms seeking WBE and WOSB certification:

- Must have a Dun & Bradstreet DUNS Number and must be registered in the System for Award Management (www.sam.gov).

CERTIFICATION PROCESS

Please note that when you click to begin the online application, you are leaving www.wbenc.org and going to a password secured, proprietary database www.wbenclink.org. Should you need to save your application and wish to return to it, make sure you return to www.wbenclink.org and use the gray box at the top right to log in. However, to register, you must use the link located at the bottom of www.wbenclink.org.

1. **Gather all of the required documents prior to beginning the online application.** For documents that do not apply to your company, please provide a written explanation stating which documents do not apply and why.
2. Review your legal and financial information to ensure that your documents support woman/women ownership and control.
3. **VERY IMPORTANT! Have the owner send a test e-mail to the database** wbenclink@cvmsolutions.com. In response, she should receive an "out-of-office" e-mail. If she does not, please have your company's IT representative ensure that e-mails from wbenclink@cvmsolutions.com can be received.
4. Register online at www.wbenc.org using the owner's contact information. The owner's complete e-mail address will be automatically assigned as the User ID for the application. Create a password. Save your user ID and password, it will be needed once certification is granted to access your profile and certificate.

5. **Complete the online certification application.** This application will become your company's résumé once certification is granted. Please type in upper and lower case letters and be as thorough as possible.

   - The application will open when registration is complete.
   - Answer ALL questions with a red asterisk to save the page.
   - Do not answer questions that are not applicable to your company.
   - If you do not know the answer to a specific question, enter an answer in the correct format that the question requires as a placeholder. You can save and return to the application to update later as long as you do not submit the application.
   - When you complete the last page of the application, the Summary View will automatically open to allow you to print the application and the Sworn Affidavit. **DO NOT SUBMIT** the application until you have reviewed it for accuracy. Once you submit, you will not be able to make changes.
   - Within 24 hours of submitting the online application, the Company Owner and Company Contact will receive an automated e-mail notification with the name of your assigned Regional Partner Organization (WBEC South), the address to mail documents, and the fee. This information also appears at the top of the printed Summary View. Contact WBEC South for the appropriate fee.

6. Mail your application processing fee, required documents, Summary View, sworn affidavit that has been signed by the female owner and notarized by a 3rd party and WBENCLink User Agreement 3.7, by certified mail, UPS or FedEx to WBEC South.

SUPPORTING DOCUMENTS
Download from www.CertAssist.net or www.wbenc.org

CONTACT
WBEC South
Attn: Certification
2800 Veterans Blvd., Suite 180
Metairie, LA 70002
Office: 504.830.0149

If you are unsure about how to answer a question on a certification application, contact a certification officer or staff member at the certifying agency, or consult a professional to ensure you understand and answer every question correctly.

U.S. DEPARTMENT OF HOUSING AND URBAN DEVELOPMENT
SECTION 3 BUSINESS

SUMMARY

CERTIFYING AGENCIES	LOCAL HUD OFFICES; NON-PROFITS; RECIPIENTS OF CERTAIN HUD FINANCIAL ASSISTANCE
DESIGNATION	SECTION 3 BUSINESS
RACE CONSCIOUS	NO
GENDER CONSCIOUS	NO
RECERTIFICATION	NONE
GRADUATION	NONE
FEE/COST	NONE
CERTIFICATION TIMEFRAME	VARIES BY AGENCY (APPROX. 30 DAYS)

OVERVIEW

The purpose of section 3 Business Certification program is to ensure that recipients of certain HUD financial assistance direct economic opportunities to Section 3 residents[1] and Section 3 business concerns. Economic opportunities include, but are not limited to, employment, apprenticeships, job training, contracts and subcontracting opportunities. HUD financial assistance covered under the Section 3 provision includes development assistance, operational assistance and modernization assistance (for example, Community Development Block Grants).

ELIGIBILITY

A business may qualify as a Section 3 business concern if:

- The business is 51% or more owned by Section 3 resident; or
- HUD Youthbuild Programs; or
- The business employs Section 3 residents for at least 30% of its full-time, permanent staff; or
- The business provides evidence of a commitment to subcontract to Section 3 business concerns, 25% or more of the dollar amount of the awarded contract.

[1]HUD Section 3 Resident (*Definition*):

- Public housing residents; or
- Persons who live in the area where a HUD-assisted project is located and who have a household income that falls below HUD's income levels for low- and very-low income individuals and households.
- **Low income:** 80% or below the median income of that area
- **Very low income:** 50% or below the median income of that area
- **Extremely low income:** 30% or below the median income of that area

Certification Process

1. Complete the HUD Section 3 Business application at www.CertAssist.net.
2. Contact the nearest HUD field office to determine where to submit your application.

Contact

HUD	Housing Authority	HUD
New Orleans Field Office	of New Orleans	**Shreveport Field Office**
Hale Boggs Federal	**DBE/WBE/Section 3 Program**	Shreveport Office Building
Building	4100 Tour St.	401 Edwards Street, Suite
500 Poydras St., 9th Floor	New Orleans, LA 70122	1510
New Orleans, LA 70130	Office: 504.670.3268	Shreveport, LA 71101-5513
Office: 504.671.3000		Office: 318.226.7030

U.S. EPARTMENT OF VETERAN AFFAIRS
SERVICE-DISABLED VETERAN-OWNED SMALL BUSINESS
VETERAN-OWNED SMALL BUSINESS

SUMMARY

CERTTIFYING AGENCY	U.S. DEPARTMENT OF VETERAN AFFAIRS
DESIGNATIONS	SDVOSB VOSB
RACE CONSCIOUS	NO
GENDER CONSCIOUS	NO
RECERTIFICATION	BI-ANNUAL
GRADUATION	NONE
FEE/COST	NONE
CERTIFICATION TIMEFRAME	INITIAL VERIFICATION: 50-90 DAYS FINAL APPROVAL: 120-180 DAYS

OVERVIEW

The Department of Veterans Affairs (VA) has special authority for Service-Disabled Veteran-Owned Small Business/Veteran-Owned Small Business (SDVOSB/VOSB) set-aside and sole source contracts Public Law (P.L.) 109-461 entitled "Veterans Benefits, Health Care, and Information Technology Act of 2006" provides VA with unique authority for contracting with SDVOSB and VOSB. A new procurement hierarchy within VA for open market procurements was created which places our highest priority with SDVOB followed by VOSB. These are followed by 8(a), HUBZone, Woman-Owned Small Business, and then all other small businesses. This procurement authority, and its subsequent implementation, is a logical extension of VA's mission, to care for our nation's Veterans. VA refers to this program as the Veterans First Contracting Program.

As a part of the VA's Veterans First Program, contract set-asides are available for Veteran Owned Small Businesses and Service Disabled Small Businesses; however, an applicant must be verified to qualify.

Verification is the process by which a Veteran is evaluated and determined eligible to be listed in the Vendor Information Pages (VIP) database. The Center for Veterans Enterprise is the office within VA that manages the verification process and verifies SDVOSB/VOSBs for inclusion in the VetBiz database. In order to qualify for participation in the VA Veterans First Contracting Program, eligible business owners must first be verified. Being verified as a SDVOSB or VOSB allows your business to participate in programs and respond to business opportunities that are only available to Veteran-owned or service-disabled Veteran-owned small businesses, once the final Veterans Affairs Acquisition Regulation (VAAR) is published.

Benefits of verification:

1. Verified firms receive priority contracting opportunities under VA's Veterans First Buying Authority;
2. Verified firms receive special consideration for Federal contracting opportunities from prime contractors and Federal government agencies;
3. Verified firms receive notices of contracting opportunities; and
4. Verified firms receive information and news affecting Veteran-Owned and Service-Disabled Veteran-Owned businesses.

ELIGIBILITY

Businesses that are owned, managed and controlled by honorably discharged veteran of the U.S. Armed Forces are eligible for participation in the VA Veterans First Contracting Program upon verification.

VERIFICATION PROCESS

1. **Create a User account** in Vendor Information Pages (VIP) to register your business with VetBiz.
2. **Enter business owner information.** You will enter business owner information, veteran status and ownership percentages if you qualify.
3. **Business owner 0877 e-Signature(s).** Business owners will be notified via e-mail that the ownership (VA Form 0877) forms are ready to be e-Signed.
4. **Enter business information.** You will enter business information and submit your business for verification.
5. **Submitted for verification.** Department of Veteran Affairs Center for Veterans Enterprise (CVE) will screen your eligibility and determine whether you have provided all required information for verification.
6. **Need additional information.** You will provide additional information for your business if you receive any requests from Department of Veterans Affairs Center for Veterans Enterprise (CVE) via e-mail.
7. **Verification.** Your business is in verification by Department of Veterans Affairs Center for Veterans Enterprise (CVE).
8. **Complete.** Your application has been completed by Department of Veterans Affairs Center for Veterans Enterprise (CVE).

CONTACT
Center for Veterans Enterprise
810 Vermont Avenue, NW
Washington, DC 20420
Toll Free: 866.584.2344
Office: 202.303.3260
vip@va.gov
www.vetbiz.gov

U.S. SMALL BUSINESS ADMINISTRATION
8(A) PROGRAM

SUMMARY

CERTTIFYING AGENCY	U.S. SMALL BUSINESS ADMINISTRATION
DESIGNATION	8(A) FIRM
RACE CONSCIOUS	NO
GENDER CONSCIOUS	NO
RECERTIFICATION	ANNUAL
GRADUATION	NINE (9) YEARS; OR
	$100 MILLION IN CONTRACTS; OR
	FIVE (5) TIMES THE VALUE OF THE COMPANY'S
	PRIMARY NAICS CODE
FEE/COST	NONE
CERTIFICATION TIMEFRAME	90-180 DAYS

OVERVIEW

In order to help small, disadvantaged businesses compete in the marketplace, the SBA created the 8(a) Business Development Program. The 8(a) Program offers a broad scope of assistance to firms that are owned and controlled at least 51% by socially and economically disadvantaged individuals. The 8(a) Program is an essential instrument for helping socially and economically disadvantaged entrepreneurs gain access to the economic mainstream of American society. The program helps thousands of aspiring entrepreneurs to gain a foothold in government contracting. Participation in the program is divided into two phases over nine years: a four-year developmental stage and a five-year transition stage.

Benefits of 8(a) certification include:

- Participants can receive sole-source contracts, up to a ceiling of $4 million for goods and services and $6.5 million for manufacturing. While the SBA helps 8(a) firms build their competitive and institutional know-how, the SBA also encourages you to participate in competitive acquisitions; and
- 8(a) firms are also able to form joint ventures and teams to bid on contracts. This enhances the ability of 8(a) firms to perform larger prime contracts and overcome the effects of contract bundling, the combining of two or more contracts together into one large contract.

ELIGIBILITY

Generally, to be approved into the 8(a) Business Development program and become certified the business must meet these eligibility requirements:

- The business must be majority-owned (51% or more) by an individual(s).
- The individual(s) must be an American citizen, by birth or naturalization.

- The business must be majority-owned (51% or more) and controlled/managed by socially and economically disadvantaged individual(s).
- The individual(s) controlling and managing the firm on a full-time basis must meet the SBA requirement for disadvantage, by proving both social disadvantage and economic disadvantage.
- The business must be a small business.
- The business must demonstrate potential for success.
- The principals must show good character.
- Separate eligibility requirements exist for a business that is owned by American Indians, Native Alaskans, Native Hawaiians or Certified Development Companies.

CERTIFICATION PROCESS

FIRST! Complete 8(a) certification training online at www.sba.gov
or through the Louisiana District Office.

1. Complete the "Is the 8(a) Business Development Program Right for My Firm?" assessment. After completing the assessment, you will know if applying for the 8(a) Business Development program is the right choice for you and your firm.
2. Get official copies of all governing documents. Articles, licenses, permits, etc. must be current and approved by your state. You must check with your state about its requirements for doing business. Bylaws, operating agreements, stock certificates, etc., must be signed by you, the owners, the officers and directors. Check with your firm's principals for the proper signatures and correct copies.
3. Obtain a free Employer Identification Number (EIN) from the Internal Revenue Service (IRS).
4. Get a free D-U-N-S number from Dun and Bradstreet (www.dnb.com).
5. Create a business profile in the System for Award Management (SAM).

NOTE: If you are having problems with EIN mismatches in SAM concerning your EIN, please contact the IRS at 1-866-255-0654 (Option 4). If you are having problems with Tax Identification Number (TIN) mismatches in SAM concerning your Social Security Number, please contact the Social Security Administration at 1-800-772-1213.

6. Get a free SBA General Login System user ID. Here's how:
- Go to SBA's General Login System
- On the left-hand side click on "Request SBA User ID"
- Create your own User ID with the following criteria:
    - At least 8 characters long
    - Contains three of the four:
        - ➢ Lowercase letter
        - ➢ Uppercase letter
        - ➢ Number

> ➢ Special character (except "&")

- Complete the SBA General Login profile
- Scroll down to "Business Information" and add your business (EIN and DUNS number) – see Step 3 – and (DUNS number) Step 4 (EIN)
- Click on the "Submit" button
- Check for an e-mail from gls@sba.gov (It will arrive immediately and contain your temporary password).
- You must change the temporary password you receive from SBA (gls@sba.gov) within 24 hours of receipt.
  - – If not changed within 24 hours, then you must request another. A second request could delay your access to the electronic application.

7. Start the free 8(a) online application
- Go to the SBA General Login system
- Select "Electronic 8(a) Certification and Annual Review System (BDMIS)"
- Select "Download & Print Authorization Form" and select "I Have Completed this Step" button
- Select "Complete Required Application Forms."
  - – Complete the 1010 Form first
  - – For each form, you must scroll down, select "Update/Complete Form", and select "Verify Completeness." This will highlight any missing data
  - – Select the "Save" button
  - – You must have green checks by each form
- Select "Return to Overview"
- Go to "Assemble Supporting Documentation"
- Select "Submit On-Line Input"
- Select "Download, Print and Sign Completed Application." This will prompt you to "Mail the Application Package, Supporting Documents and Checklist to the SBA"
- Once you have mailed the documents to SBA, login and select "I have mailed the package…." This puts your application in the queue for processing so an SBA analyst can begin the review process. Only two SBA offices receive and process applications for the 8(a) Business Development program (California and Pennsylvania). Follow the instructions on the application carefully. For questions on where to send the application, contact 8aquestions@sba.gov.

The hard copy of the SBA 8(A) application is available online at www.CertAssist.net.

CONTACT
Louisiana District Office of the U.S. Small Business Administration
365 Canal Street, Suite 2820
New Orleans, LA 70130
Office: 504.589.6685
www.sba.gov

- For general questions about the 8(a) Business Development program, please contact **8aquestions@sba.gov**
- For help with SBA's General Login System, contact **GLS@sba.gov**
- For help with SAM, which replaced the Central Contractor Registration, please go to **sam.gov** or **fsd.gov**
- For help with the 8(a) online application, please e-mail **BDMIS@sba.gov**
- For help with 8(a) regulations and requirements, please e-mail **8aBD@sba.gov**

SBA 8(a) Certification Workshop

Every 2nd Wednesday of the month

10:00am CST

SBA Louisiana District Office
365 Canal Street
New Orleans, LA 70130

U.S. SMALL BUSINESS ADMINISTRATION
WOMEN-OWNED SMALL BUSINESS & ECONOMICALLY DISADVANTAGED WOMEN-OWNED SMALL BUSINESS

SUMMARY

CERTTIFYING AGENCY	**U.S. SMALL BUSINESS ADMINISTRATION**
DESIGNATIONS	WOSB EDWOSB
RACE CONSCIOUS	NO
GENDER CONSCIOUS	YES
RECERTIFICATION	ANNUAL
GRADUATION	NONE
FEE/COST	NONE
CERTIFICATION TIMEFRAME	60-120 DAYS

OVERVIEW

On October 7, 2010, the U.S. Small Business Administration published a final rule effective February 4, 2011, aimed at expanding Federal contracting opportunities for women-owned small businesses (WOSBs). The Women-Owned Small Business (WOSB) Federal Contract program authorizes contracting officers to set aside certain Federal contracts for eligible:

- Women-owned small businesses (WOSBs) or
- Economically disadvantaged women-owned small businesses (EDWOSBs)

The WOSB Federal Contracting Program provides greater access to Federal contracting opportunities for WOSBs and EDWOSBs. The program allows contracting offices, for the first time, to set-aside specific contracts for certified WOSBs and EDWOSBs and will help Federal agencies achieve the existing statutory goal of five percent (5%) of Federal contracting dollars be awarded to women-owned businesses.

ELIGIBILITY

To be eligible for certification as a WOSB, a firm must be at least 51% owned and controlled by one or more women, and primarily managed by one or more women. The women must be U.S. citizens. The firm must be "small" in its primary industry in accordance with SBA's size standards for that industry. In order for a WOSB to be deemed "economically disadvantaged," its owners must demonstrate economic disadvantage in accordance with the requirements set forth in the final rule.

CERTIFICATION PROCESS

The SBA has approved four organizations to act as Third Party Certifiers under the WOSB Program. The four organizations and contact information are:

- El Paso Hispanic Chamber of Commerce

- National Women Business Owners Corporation
- US Women's Chamber of Commerce
- Women's Business Enterprise National Council (WBENC)

Women Owned Small Businesses may elect to use the services of a Third Party Certifier to demonstrate eligibility for the program, or they may self-certify using the process outlined on the SBA website. SBA will only accept third party certification from these entities, and firms are still subject to the same eligibility requirements to participate in the program. Please note, at the request of WBENC, SBA has approved WBENC only for the certification of WOSBs and not for the certification of Economically Disadvantaged WOSBs.

1. Read the WOSB Compliance Guide (available at www.CertAssist.net or online at www.sba.gov).
2. Register and represent your status in www.sam.gov as a WOSB or EDWOSB.
3. Register in the SBA's General Login System (GLS). Once you are in GLS, click the "Access" button at the top of the screen. Then select "Women-Owned Small Business Program Repository" and press submit. You should then be able to access the repository. Once you are in the repository, you can click the "Help" button at the top of the screen for instructions on how to use the repository. A complete list of required documents to upload to the Repository can be found in the WOSB Compliance Guide.

CONTACT
Louisiana District Office
U.S. Small Business Administration
365 Canal Street, Suite 2820
New Orleans, LA 70130
Office: 504.589.6685
www.sba.gov

- For general questions about the 8(a) Business Development program, please contact **wosb@sba.gov**
- For help with SBA's General Login System, contact **GLS@sba.gov**
- For help with SAM, which replaced the Central Contractor Registration, please go to **sam.gov** or **fsd.gov**

SBA Answer Desk
1-800-U-ASK-SBA 1-800-827-5722
Answer Desk TTY: (704) 344-6640
[Spanish]
E-mail: wosb@sba.gov

U.S. SMALL BUSINESS ADMINISTRATION
HUBZONE

SUMMARY

CERTTIFYING AGENCY	U.S. SMALL BUSINESS ADMINISTRATION
DESIGNATION	HUBZONE FIRM
RACE CONSCIOUS	NO
GENDER CONSCIOUS	NO
RECERTIFICATION	TRI-ANNUAL (3) YEARS
GRADUATION	NONE
FEE/COST	NONE
CERTIFICATION TIMEFRAME	30-90 DAYS

OVERVIEW

The **Historically Underutilized Business Zones** (HUBZone) program encourages economic development in historically underutilized business zones - "HUBZones" - through the establishment of preferences. SBA's HUBZone program is in line with the efforts of both the Administration and Congress to promote economic development and employment growth in distressed areas by providing access to more Federal contracting opportunities. The SBA regulates and implements the HUBZone program by:

- Determining which businesses are eligible to receive HUBZone contracts;
- Maintaining a listing of qualified HUBZone businesses that Federal agencies can use to locate vendors;
- Adjudicating protests of eligibility to receive HUBZone contracts; and
- Reporting to Congress on the program's employment and investment impact in HUBZone areas.

The program's benefits for HUBZone-certified companies include:

- Competitive and sole source contracting;
- 10% price evaluation preference in full and open contract competitions, as well as subcontracting opportunities; and
- The Federal government's goal of awarding 3% of all dollars for Federal prime contracts to HUBZone-certified small business concerns.

ELIGIBILITY

To qualify for the program, a business, except tribally owned concerns, must be a small business for its primary NAICS code and it must meet one of the following ownership and control requirements:

- Owned and controlled at least 51% by U.S. citizens
- Wholly owned or owned in party by one or more Indian Tribal Governments or by a corporation that is wholly owned by one or more Indian Tribal Governments

- An American Native Corporation (ANC) owned and controlled by Natives or a direct or indirect subsidiary corporation, joint venture, or partnership of an ANC
- Wholly or owned in part by a Community Development Corporation (CDC)
- A small agricultural cooperative or a small business concern wholly owned or owned in party by one or more small agricultural cooperatives
- Except for certain concerns owned by Indian Tribal Governments, all other small businesses must have a principal office located in a qualified HUBZone
- At least 35% of all of its employees must reside in a HUBZone. Reside means to live in a primary residence at a place for at least 180 days, or as a currently registered voter, and with intent to live there indefinitely.

Firms that are owned in whole or in part by Indian Tribal Governments or corporations wholly owned by Indian tribal Governments, at the time of application must either:

- Maintain a principal office located in a HUBZone and ensure that at least 35% of its employees reside in a HUBZone; or
- Certify that when performing a HUBZone contract, at least 35% of its employees engaged in performing that contract will reside within any Indian reservation governed by one or more of the Indian Tribal Government owners, or reside within any HUBZone adjoining such Indian reservation. A HUBZone and Indian reservation are adjoining when the two areas are next to and in contact with each other; and the concern will "attempt to maintain" the applicable employment percentage stated above during the performance of any HUBZone contract it receives.

CERTIFICATION PROCESS
1. There are several important registrations that must be completed before you can start the electronic application process:

- The firm must have an Employer Identification Number/Tax Identification Number (EIN/TIN).
- DUN & BRADSTREET: Each headquarters and branch office must be registered so that it will have its own DNB DUNS Number.
- System for Award Management (SAM): NOTE- the principal office address that is applying for HUBZone certification must be entered in the SAM profile associated with DUNS appropriate for this specific physical location.
- Dynamic Small Business Search (DSBS), aka, SBA's supplemental page: DSBS profiles will reflect each firm's certification status. It is recommended to keep your profiles (SAM and DSBS page) up to date through the SAM website. At the SAM Web site, simply update your SAM profile and SAM will update the DSBS profile. (NOTE: edit updated data transferred from SAM to DSBS usually takes up to 24 hours after you have updated the SAM profile.)

- General Login System (GLS): you must complete registration in this system for each individual that can update information to your concern. Once you have registered, then you must add the concern's DUNS and EIN number(s).
2. Review the list of supporting documentation you will need to submit to your Business Opportunity Specialist after submitting the online application. See the supporting documentation request for detailed descriptions of acceptable versions of these documents.

3. Signed HUBZone Program Certification Signature Sheet (see Related Forms, below)
    a. Principal office location lease/rental agreement and utility bill
    b. Last 3 years of business tax returns, including all schedules and attachments
    c. Most recent personal Federal tax returns for all owners, including all schedules and attachments
    d. Citizenship documentation of business owners that are U.S. Citizens

    - For Corporations:
        i. Articles of Incorporation
        ii. Copies of all stock certificates (front and back), and stock ledger
        iii. Corporate Bylaws and any amendments
        iv. Certificate of Good Standing

    - For Limited Liability Companies (LLC):
        i. Operating Agreement and any amendments
        ii. Articles of Organizations and any amendments
        iii. Certificate of Good Standing

    - For Partnerships:
        I. Partnership Agreement and any amendments
        II. Official payroll record
        III. HUBZone maps of employees' home addresses
        IV. Most recent State Unemployment tax filing/report
        V. Valid (unexpired) Driver's License, DMV ID or voter registration cards for each employee residing in a HUBZone

CONTACT
Louisiana District Office
U.S. Small Business Administration
365 Canal Street, Suite 2820
New Orleans, LA 70130
Office: 504.589.6685
www.sba.gov

- For general questions about the 8(a) Business Development program, please contact **hubzone@sba.gov**
- For help with SBA's General Login System, contact **GLS@sba.gov**
- For help with SAM, which replaced the Central Contractor Registration, please go to **sam.gov** or **fsd.gov**
- Search to see if your business is in a HUBZone below:

http://map.sba.gov/hubzone/maps/

LOUISIANA PROCURMENT TECHNICAL ASSISTANCE CENTERS

SUMMARY

CERTTIFYING AGENCY	**LOUISIANA PROCUREMENT TECHNICAL ASSISTANCE CENTER**
DESIGNATION	LA PTAC CLIENT
RACE CONSCIOUS	NO
GENDER CONSCIOUS	NO
RECERTIFICATION	NONE
GRADUATION	NONE
FEE/COST	NONE
CERTIFICATION TIMEFRAME	10-30 DAYS

OVERVIEW

The Louisiana Procurement Technical Assistance Center (LA PTAC) was established in 1989 to increase Federal, state and local government contracting awards to companies located in Louisiana. LA PTAC's goal is to strengthen the competitive position of Louisiana businesses and industries. LA PTAC provides a wide range of assistance, most free of charge, to businesses through one-on-one counseling sessions, classes, seminars and matchmaking events, including:

Determining Suitability for Contracting: The government marketplace poses unique challenges that can overwhelm or even ruin a company that does not have the maturity or resources to meet them. LA PTAC counselors can help you determine if your company is ready for government opportunities as well as how to best position your company for success.

Securing Necessary Registrations: LA PTAC can help make sure you are registered with the databases necessary for you to participate in the government marketplace, including Dun and Bradstreet and SAM.GOV.

Researching Procurement Histories: What agencies have bought products like yours in the past? Which companies have been awarded these contracts? How much have they been paid? Answers to questions like these are necessary to guide your marketing strategy and give your company a competitive edge. LAPTAC can help you ask the right questions and get the information you need to succeed.

Networking: LA PTAC sponsors "matchmaking" events, providing critical opportunities to connect with agency buying officers, prime contractors and other businesses that may offer teaming or subcontracting opportunities.

Identifying Bid Opportunities: LA PTAC can make sure that you are notified -- on a daily basis -- of all government contract opportunities that your company is eligible to bid.

Proposal Preparation: An LA PTAC procurement specialist can help you navigate even the most difficult solicitation package, including securing necessary specifications and drawings and determining pricing. You will never need to pass up a great contract opportunity just because the solicitation is too complicated.

Contract Performance Issues: Even after you have been awarded a contract, LA PTAC may be able to help with certain contract performance issues, such as:

- Negotiating and interfacing with the agency;
- Developing a cost-accounting system;
- Bonding and interim financing; and
- Developing environmental, quality control and accident prevention plans.

Preparing for Audit: When it is time for your contract audit, LA PTAC can make sure you know what to expect, and what you will need to have all documentation in order.

ELIGIBILITY
LA PTAC provides procurement technical assistance to **ALL** small and large Louisiana-based businesses.

CERTIFICATION PROCESS
1. Obtain a DNB DUNS Number and register your business in www.sam.gov.
2. Download the LA PTAC Client Profile and Search Profile forms from www.CertAssist.net.
3. Complete the **LA PTAC Client Profile Form** and the **LA PTAC Search Profile Information Form.**
4. Return the forms to the LA PTAC State Program Office.

CONTACT
LA PTAC STATE PROGRAM OFFICE
Louisiana PTAC
http://www.la-ptac.org
University of Louisiana - Lafayette
University of Louisiana
PO Box 44172
Lafayette, LA 70504-4172
Phone: (337) 482-6422

Additional LA PTAC contacts appear on the following page.

CONTACTS

LA PTAC STATE PROGRAM OFFICE
Louisiana PTAC
http://www.la-ptac.org
University of Louisiana - Lafayette
University of Louisiana
PO Box 44172
Lafayette, LA 70504-4172
Phone: (337) 482-6422

Sherrie Mullins
Program Manager
Phone: (337) 482-6422
E-mail: sbm3321@louisiana.edu

Peggy Sammons
Administrative Staff
Phone: (337) 482-6422
E-mail: prs6182@louisiana.edu

Dianna Romero
Administrative Staff
Phone: (337) 482-6422
E-mail: dxm1479@louisiana.edu

Cindy Carrier
Procurement Counselor
Phone: (337) 482-6422
E-mail: cindycarrier@me.com

Sheila Wallace
Procurement Counselor
Phone: (337) 482-6422
E-mail: kdptac@kricket.net

NW LA REGIONAL PTAC OFFICE
NW Louisiana Government
Procurement Center
http://www.nwlagpc.org

Shreveport Chamber of Commerce
400 Edwards Street
Shreveport, LA 71101
Phone: (318) 677-2532

Kelly Ford
PTAC Program Manager
E-mail: kelly@shreveportchamber.org

Jennifer Whittington
Procurement Technical Assistant
Phone: (318) 677-2530
E-mail: jennifer@shreveportchamber.org

Michael Haire
Procurement Counselor
Phone: (318) 677-2529
E-mail: mike@shreveportchamber.org

Jeanene Deen
Procurement Counselor
Phone: (318) 677-2519
E-mail: jeanene@shreveportchamber.org

Do not rely on your DBE status alone to win contracts. Rely, instead, on creating, capturing and delivering value for your potential clients and partners. Market your status as a certified DBE, SBE, MBE and/or WBE firm as lagniappe.

Lagniappe (def.)
1. Something extra.
2. A bonus.

(Origin: Louisiana French Creole circa 1844)

GENERAL SERVICES ADMINISTRATION SCHEDULES

The GSA Schedules program is the premier acquisition vehicle in government, with approximately $50 billion a year in spending or 10% of overall Federal procurement spending.

GSA Schedules are fast, easy, and effective contracting vehicles for both customers and vendors. For GSA Schedules, GSA establishes long-term, government-wide contracts with commercial companies to provide access to millions of commercial products and services at volume discount pricing.

GSA is always looking to update the offerings under the GSA Schedules program and aid vendors in being successful in the government marketplace. Particularly, the GSA Schedules program has a strong record of small business achievement. In Fiscal Year 2011, 35%, or approximately $13 billion in prime contracting, went to small business.

To be successful under the GSA Schedules program, vendors should be prepared to take necessary steps to be productive in a highly competitive marketplace. Having a GSA Schedule contract is a significant investment on the part of the vendor and GSA. Careful analysis, planning, and proactive steps are required to ensure vendors are successful under the GSA Schedules program.

GSA is committed to helping vendors succeed in the government marketplace. To aid you with your decision to get on a GSA Schedule, here is some important information to consider:

- Eighty percent (80%) of GSA Multiple Award Schedule (MAS) contractors are small businesses who represent 36% of sales;
- More than $40B flows through GSA MAS contracts every year;
- In Fiscal Year 2012, approximately 10% of government needs were procured through the GSA MAS contracts;
- GSA had over 19,000 MAS contracts in Fiscal Year 2012; and,
- Approximately 40 percent of the 19,000 GSA MAS contracts generate sales.

GSA has developed the Vendor Toolbox, which is a collection of resources that will ultimately help you decide whether getting a GSA Schedule contract is in your best interests.

GSA Vendor Toolbox: https://vsc.gsa.gov/RA/

Source: www.gsa.gov

SAMPLE CHECKLIST OF SUPPORTING DOCUMENTS

Articles of Incorporation or Organization
Letter of Good Standing from the Louisiana Secretary of State or Secretary of State or agency where the business is domiciled
Corporate Bylaws or LLC Operating Agreement
Current license to do business in Louisiana (Parish business license)
Copy of trade license(s) held by the firm and/or firm owner(s)
List all business names previously used by any owner
Stock ownership options, or agreements between owners, which restrict the DBE ownership or control of the owners
Stock Transfer Ledger and Certificates- Front and Back (Corporations Only)
Type of stock- Common and/or Preferred and the number of shares of each that are currently outstanding, along with the total number of shares authorized to be issued by the corporation
Membership Transfer Ledger and Certificates- Front and Back (LLCs Only)
Member ownership options, or agreements between members, which restrict the DBE/EDB membership or control of the members
Indicate the total number of Membership Certificates outstanding and authorized to be issued by the company
List of all persons in the firm currently working for any other business which has a relation with the applicant firm
Business Balance Sheet (< 90-days old)
Business Income Statement (<90-days old)
Personal Financial Statement (<90-days old)
Signed copies of Federal business tax returns for the last three (3) years
Signed copies of Federal personal tax returns for the past three (3) years
Business Organizational Chart
Résumés of owners, officers, and key personnel
Proof of U.S. Citizenship (e.g., Driver's License, State Issued ID, Passport)
Bank signature card for the primary business bank account
Document(s) reflecting each owner's share of profits, losses and ownership
Document(s) indicating the initial and subsequent capitalization of the firm by the owner(s)
Certificates of title for all equipment owned by the company
Copies of any loans or lines of credit from the business to any owner or member of the firm
Confidential statement(s) relative to each denial of a business loan, business line of credit, personal loan for the business, and/or unfair treatment for the applicant
Confidential statement(s) relative to each denial of a business opportunity and/or unfair treatment against the business
Documentation confirming a disability of the DBE/SBE applicant owner(s)

Note: Supporting documentation requirements vary by certification program. Visit **www.CertAssist.net/certification-toolkit** for free DBE certification supporting document templates and forms

PROCUREMENT & BUSINESS DEVELOPMENT RESOURCES

WWW.FBO.GOV

Federal Business Opportunities (FedBizOpps) is a web-based system for posting solicitations and other procurement-related documents to the Internet. FedBizOpps was designated by the Federal Acquisition Regulation as the mandatory government wide point of entry for the posting of government business opportunities greater than $25,000. FedBizOpps allows contract specialists throughout the Federal government to post synopses and other procurement documents, such as solicitations, amendments, and award notifications to a common index. This index, accessible on the FedBizOpps web site, allows vendors to search databases containing information from many Federal agencies. Vendors may also subscribe to FedBizOpps to receive daily e-mail notifications of requirements and procurement announcements.

LAPAC | HTTPS://WWWPRD1.DOA.LOUISIANA.GOV/OSP/LAPAC/PUBMAIN.CFM

The Louisiana Procurement and Contract Network (LAPAC) is the State of Louisiana's central portal for posting bids and request for proposal (RFPs) solicitations and contract award information on the internet.

WWW.SBA.GOV

The U.S. Small Business Administration (SBA) is an independent agency of the U.S. Federal government created to aid, counsel, assist and protect the interests of small business concerns through:

- Access to capital
- Entrepreneurial development
- Government contracting
- Small business advocacy

WWW.SCORE.ORG

SCORE is a nonprofit organization with over 13,000 volunteers who help small businesses start, grow and succeed nationwide by providing confidential business counseling to entrepreneurs at no charge.

WWW.ASBDC-US.ORG

The Association of Small Business Development Centers has over 1,000 service centers throughout the U.S., Guam, American Samoa, Puerto Rico and the U.S. Virgin Islands that provide no-cost business consulting and low-cost training for America's small businesses.

WWW.MBDA.GOV

The Minority Business Development Agency (MBDA), a part of the U.S. Department of Commerce, is an entrepreneurially focused Federal agency with a mission to actively promote the growth and competitiveness of large, medium and small minority business enterprises (MBEs) in the U.S.

WWW.HUD.GOV

The purpose of *HUD's Small Business Resource Guide* is to provide a compendium of practical information on national, state and local small business resources which assist individuals who are about to start or expand a business. In addition to providing basic information on existing small businesses programs and contracting with the Federal government, there is specific guidance on contracting with the Department of Housing and Urban Development (HUD) and the contracting opportunities available with HUD grantees.

WWW.ANNUALCREDITREPORT.COM

This central Federal government website allows you to request a free personal credit file disclosure, commonly called a credit report, once every 12 months from each of the nationwide consumer credit reporting companies: Equifax, Experian and TransUnion.

WWW.DNB.COM

Dun & Bradstreet is the world's leading provider of business credit reports and the business credit bureau that can assist you in establishing a business credit profile.

WWW.TRADE.GOV

The U.S. Commercial Service is the trade promotion arm of the U.S. Department of Commerce's International Trade Administration. U.S. Commercial Service trade professionals in over 100 U.S. cities and in more than 75 countries help U.S. companies get started in exporting or increase sales to new global markets.

WWW.CENSUS.GOV

The U.S. Census Bureau's website provides up-to-date statistical data on the U.S. population, U.S. business and industry and the U.S. economy.

WWW.APTAC-US.ORG

Operating through Procurement Technical Assistance Centers in the U.S., Guam and Puerto Rico, the Procurement Technical Assistance Program helps businesses compete for Federal, state and local government contracting opportunities by providing them with expert consulting services at little or no charge.

WWW.SBA.GOV/CONTENT/WOMENS-BUSINESS-CENTERS

The U.S. Small Business Administration's Women's Business Center Program consists of Women's Business Resource Centers in the U.S. and Puerto Rico that provide business training, counseling and resources to help women and men start and grow successful businesses.

WWW.EXPORT.GOV

Export.gov helps businesses plan their international sales strategies and overcome challenges of global market access and trade compliance.

WWW.VETBIZ.GOV
VETBIZ.GOV is the U.S. Department of Veteran Affair's website that is dedicated to helping veterans of the armed forces start and grow successful businesses.

WWW.REGULATIONS.GOV
Regulations.gov is the U.S. government's online source for up-to-date regulations from nearly 300 Federal agencies.

WWW.USA.GOV
USA.gov provides access to every Federal agency website as well as to state websites and local consumer and business resources.

WWW.NWBC.GOV
The National Women's Business Council is a bi-partisan Federal advisory council created to serve as an independent source of advice and counsel to the President, Congress, and the U.S. Small Business Administration on economic issues of importance to women business owners.

WWW.NIST.GOV/MEP/ (MANUFACTURING EXTENSION PARTNERSHIP)
The National Institute of Standards and Technology's Hollings Manufacturing Extension Partnership (MEP) works with small and mid-sized U.S. manufacturers to help them create and retain jobs, increase profits, and save time and money.

WWW.NMSDC.ORG
The National Minority Supplier Development Council certifies and matches minority owned businesses with over 3,600 member corporations that want to purchase goods and services.

WWW.WBENC.ORG
The Women's Business Enterprise National Council is the largest third-party certifier of businesses owned controlled, and operated by women in the United States.

WWW.USCHAMBER.COM
The U.S. Chamber of Commerce is the world's largest business federation representing the interests of more than 3 million businesses of all sizes, sectors and regions. There are also national, regional and local chambers for specific ethnic groups:

- **WWW.USWCC.ORG**
  U.S. Women's Chamber of Commerce

- **WWW.NATIONALBCC.ORG**
  National Black Chamber of Commerce

- **WWW.USPAAC.COM**
  U.S. Pan Asian Chamber of Commerce

- **WWW.USHCC.ORG**
  U.S. Hispanic Chamber of Commerce

- **WWW.NGLCC.ORG**
  National Gay & Lesbian Chamber of Commerce

WWW.GRANTS.GOV
Grants.gov is the free central portal of the U.S. government where you can find and apply for all Federal grant opportunities.

WWW.SAM.GOV
Anyone seeking to do business with the Federal government must register with the System for Award Management

The #1 resource on the Internet for information on Louisiana small business certification programs, training and resources

OUR COMPANY

Start Smart is a national provider of consulting, training and publishing products and services for government, private and non-profit organizations.

At Start Smart, we recognize that while many clients have similar challenges, each client has unique needs. By taking a holistic, strategic and analytical approach to addressing those needs, we shed new insights about our clients to help them improve organizational performance and realize tangible bottom-line results. Our clients rely on our deep expertise and the combined capabilities of our exceptional people to help them build better organizations.

Our Mission
We are dedicated to helping our clients build more competitive and higher-performing organizations.

Our Values
Ethical, honest, trustworthy, respectful and responsible are the values by which we operate. As a result, we will engage in no transaction that does not benefit all parties involved.

OUR PRACTICE AREAS

Supplier Diversity Consulting
Our supplier diversity consultants help organizations improve supplier participation by small businesses (SBEs), disadvantaged businesses (DBEs), veteran owned small businesses (SDVOSBs/VOSBs), minority-owned businesses (MBEs) and women-owned businesses (WBEs) through our proactive, high engagement consulting approach.

From program development and compliance management to supplier outreach and training, the bottom line effect is two-fold: (1) Start Smart can help organizations increase supply chain and contract participation by historically underutilized businesses; and (2) as a certified MBE/DBE/SBE firm, the cost of our services may be counted towards an organization's diversity spend and goals.

Training
We offer clients a total training solution through our inventory business management, leadership and financial empowerment seminars, workshops and training programs

aligned with our core practice areas. Our training programs can be delivered by one of our highly skilled instructors or as a turnkey solution. Because we own all of our intellectual property, we can develop flexible and customized solutions for each client's specific training needs.

Publishing

At Start Smart, we believe in the adage, "publish or perish". That is why we take our expertise and what we learn in the field to publish books and learning programs delivered through multiple learning platforms for entrepreneurs and organizations and those who want to help them succeed. Our book, *Principles of Building Business Credit*, has remained one of the best-selling books in America on building business credit since its first edition publication in 2009.

Our current publishing catalog includes:

Books
- Principles of Building Business Credit
- Ultimate Strategy: How to Write a One Page Strategic Business Plan
- Ultimate Planning: The Ultimate Business Plan Planner
- Louisiana Business Certifications Guidebook
- Construction Laborer Job Readiness Assessment

Training and Home Study Programs
- Contractor's College® construction business management training program
- Ultimate Business Planning System® business planning home study program

Visit our website to learn more about our company, services and products:

www.StartSmartLLC.com

Contractor's Bootcamp® is an intensive, two-day construction business management training program that empowers emerging contractors to compete with confidence in the highly competitive construction industry.

Contractor's Bootcamp® Curriculum

The core curriculum is designed to help emerging contractors improve their businesses in the four major areas of consideration of project owners, banks, surety and insurance companies- *Capacity, Credibility, Capital* and *Credit.*

Day 1
- Strategic Business Planning for Contractors
- Success through Business Certifications
- Credit Smart Contractor: Building Business Credit
- Introduction to Financial Statements
- Accessing Capital for Growth
- Writing a Clear, Concise & Powerful Capability Statement

Day 2
- Introduction to Surety Bonds
- Insurance & Risk Management for Contractors
- How to Respond to Bids & RFPs
- Capstone: Construction Project Management

Why choose Contractor's Bootcamp®?
- Award-winning program
- Over 550 contractors trained
- Over $100 million in surety bonding secured by graduates
- Over $70 million in contracts secured by graduates

E-mail Training@StartSmartLLC.com to learn more about the program, to license our curriculum or to have our team of experts conduct the program for emerging contractors in your community.

CONRACTOR'S COLLEGE

CONSTRUCTION LABORER
JOB READINESS ASSESSMENT

The Construction Laborer Job Readiness Assessment is a cognitive examination of the basic knowledge and skills required for an individual to perform as a laborer or helper on any construction site.

The assessment is designed to improve the process of recruiting, hiring, training and retaining quality low-skilled construction workers.

www.ContractorsCollege.com